Time's Language

Selected Poems

(1959-2018)

Margaret Randall

by Elaine de Kooning, 1960.

Elaine de Kooning, as was often her custom, signed and dated
this portrait decades after it was finished. It was actually
painted in 1960. Randall was pregnant with her son at the time
of the sitting and moved to Mexico shortly afterwards, in 1961.

Time's Language

Selected Poems

(1959-2018)

Margaret Randall

Edited by
Katherine M. Hedeen and Víctor Rodríguez Núñez

WingsPress

San Antonio, Texas

2018

Time's Language: Selected Poems (1959-2018)
© 2018 by Margaret Randall

Cover art: "Hummingbird" by Liliana Wilson.

First Edition

ISBN: 978-1-60940-573-1 (Hardback/cloth)

E-books:

epub: 978-1-60940-574-8
Mobipocket/Kindle: 978-1-60940-575-5
Library PDF: 978-1-60940-576-2

Wings Press
P.O. Box 591176
San Antonio, TX 78259

wingspresspublishing@gmail.com

Wings Press books are distributed to the trade by
Independent Publishers Group
www.ipgbook.com

Library of Congress Cataloging-in-Publication Data:

Names: Randall, Margaret, 1936- author. | Hedeen, Katherine M. 1971-
editor.| Rodríguez Núñez, Víctor, 1955- editor.
Title: Time's language : selected poems, (1959-2018) / Margaret Randall ;
  edited by Katherine M. Hedeen and Víctor Rodríguez Núñez,.
Description: First edition. | San Antonio, Texas : Wings Press, 2018. |
  Includes bibliographical references.
Identifiers: LCCN 2018002033| ISBN 9781609405731 (cloth/hard-
back : alk. paper) | ISBN 9781609405755 (mobipocket/kindle) | ISBN
9781609405762 (pdf) | 9781609405748 (ePub)

Classification: LCC PS3535.A56277 A6 2018 | DDC 811/.54--dc23
LC record available at https://lccn.loc.gov/2018002033

Contents

From *The Coming Home Poems*
(East Haven: LongRiver Books, 1986)

From *Memory Says Yes*
(Willimantic, CT: Curbstone Press, 1988)

From *Dancing with the Doe: New and Selected Poems, 1986-1991*
(Albuquerque: New End Press, 1992)

From *Hunger's Table: Women, Food and Politics*
(Watsonville, CA: Papier-Mâché Press, 1997)

From *Where They Left You for Dead*
(Boulder: EdgeWork Books, 2002)

From *Halfway Home*
(Boulder: EdgeWork Books, 2002)

From *Into Another Time: Grand Canyon Reflections*
(Albuquerque: West End Press, 2004)

From *Stones Witness*
(Tucson: University of Arizona Press, 2007)

From *She Becomes Time*
(San Antonio: Wings Press, 2016)

From *The Morning After: Poetry and Prose in a Post-Truth World*
(San Antonio: Wings Press, 2017)

Uncollected Poems

Photographs

Margaret Randall's Commitment to Poetry

Ultimately, there are two kinds of poets: those who have a long *vitae* and those who have an amazing life. Just glancing at Margaret Randall's list of works is enough to show us we are before a distinguished and prolific writer. Beginning with *Giant of Tears* in 1959, she has published over forty poetry collections. To this we can add dozens more—works of oral history, essays, photography, translations, and anthologies—for a total of approximately one hundred books, many of which have been translated into Bengali, Bulgarian, Dutch, French, German, Italian, Japanese, Portuguese, Slovenian, Turkish, and for over four decades, Spanish. Yet this impressive catalog of publications pales in comparison to her life.

Randall was born in New York City on December 6, 1936 to an upper middle class Jewish family. When she was ten, her parents set out on a journey through the country searching for better horizons. After two months, they arrived in New Mexico and, fascinated by the physical and human landscape, settled in Albuquerque. In this city—surrounded by the desert and a strong Indigenous and Hispanic presence—Randall grew up and studied. In 1954, a recent high school graduate, she married for the first time and traveled by motorcycle throughout Northern Africa and Europe, ending up in Seville, Spain. She remained there until 1956, working odd jobs that included everything from being a maid to a bullfight reporter. Most importantly, she began to learn Spanish.

In 1957, having returned to the States, she divorced—"[i]t was a bad marriage, only a way to escape"—and moved back to New York. There she completed her intellectual formation, always at the margins of the academy, and defined her vocation as a writer. She also began to acquire a radical social consciousness. She wrote her first notable poems, reading in cafes and publishing in small literary magazines. She was associated with both the Beats and the Black Mountain poets. In 1960, her first child, Gregory, was born—"it was a wanted pregnancy, but being a single mother in those days wasn't very common."

A year later, "New York had nothing more to offer," and Randall left with her son for Mexico. There she met various poets, including Nicaraguan Ernesto Cardenal, Peruvian Raquel Jodorowsky, Mexican Juan Bañuelos, and American Philip Lamantia. In the environment they shared, "the American poets realized that the Latin Americans knew nothing of our poetic history and that we knew nothing of theirs." To challenge this, she founded in Mexico, in 1962, *The Plumed Horn/ El corno emplumado,* a bilingual journal that, until its disappearance in 1969, published thirty-one volumes of more than two hundred pages each, and some twenty books by North American and South American authors. It was a shared adventure, first with the Mexican poet Sergio Mondragón, and later with the American poet Robert Cohen. In Mexico her three daughters were born: Sarah (1963), Ximena (1964), and Ana (1969).

The Plumed Horn/ El corno emplumado was a victim of the Mexican government's repression against the student movement of the time, and Randall was forced to live underground and even leave the country illegally. After a journey in which she traveled half way around the world, in the fall of 1969 she arrived in Havana, where her four children awaited her. She lived there until 1980. In Cuba, she worked at the Book Institute, was a jury member for the Casa de las Américas Prize, and wrote for cultural publications. She also traveled—with Cuban documents since the United States and Mexico denied them to her—to Chile (1972), Peru (end of 1973 and beginning of 1974), and Vietnam (1974, six months before the end of the war). Yet the last years in Cuba were not easy—"I never knew why they didn't let me work and at the same time paid my salary."

Randall visited Nicaragua in 1979 after the Sandinista Revolution. Finally having regained her Mexican passport, she settled there a year later. These were "intense and interesting times of participation." In 1983, after having lived almost a quarter century in Latin America, she began to feel the "need to go back home." The return to the United States became a reality in 1984. After receiving a year-long visa, she applied for residency, planning on recovering her citizenship. But her request was denied. In October 1985 she was ordered deported; and she, as we might expect, decided to fight the decision. The first hearing was in March 1986 and the last in August 1989, when, after having lost every prior appeal, she was finally successful.

Undoubtedly, we are before a truly tireless, unshakable woman. Randall has raised four children—who have now given her ten grandchildren and two great grandchildren—has realized intense radical political activism, and hasn't stopped writing and translating for an instant. Currently, along with her creative work she gives lectures and readings and collaborates with journals and newspapers. She lives in Albuquerque with her partner, the painter Barbara Byers. She has written: "I began therapy that helped me to remember that I was the victim of incest as a child, and once I began to understand my sexual identity I was able to recognize and accept the fact that I am a lesbian." For many years she wrote at the foot of the Sandia Mountains and recently moved to a smaller home in town.

Randall's journals will undoubtedly be a much-read work. Selections have already been published in *Albuquerque: Coming Back to the U.S.A.* (New Star Books, 1986) and *To Change the World: My Years in Cuba* (Rutgers, 2009). Certainly, the best pages of her biography are her poems, since the intense life she has lead, and that we've briefly presented, are gathered there. She has insisted that poetic creation, which "spans everything," is nothing more than "pure experience, life at its fullest." Something more than life or death, "always and fundamentally a risk, never a string of words that describe something." She also believes that "we are all born poets" and that the societies in which we live kill that creativity. "As a poet, lover, mother, educator, and activist, I always struggle against this."

In the fight against the dehumanization that defines, in her opinion, much of contemporary poetic practice, the recuperation of memory is fundamental. And hers is full and constantly giving birth, from childhood portraits to family snapshots, yet with a critical eye, for her daily struggle against oblivion does not commit idealizations. Her combing through memory is nothing short of a search for identity that is manifest as political, national, gender, ethnic, and sexual. The result is an active, participative poetic subject, constantly seeking to transform all that is unjust.

For Randall, the recuperation of other people's experiences is as important as that of her own human condition. Her poetic voice only reaches its definition in relationship with the other, who ultimately has its own voice. Thus, she contributes in some way to the liberation of us all. In particular, she vindicates the right of women to express themselves. That is why she defines her poems as "a vehicle for others' voices, above all, for those women who, due to a variety of circumstances, have not been heard before." These poems crossed with other voices, are in her opinion, those of a "committed poet. I've never fled from the term, which I'm proud of. I am committed to life, my condition as a woman and human being, and that is why I'm committed to poetry."

In Randall's poetry, North and South American traditions are fused. The first important poets for her were "those who sought an American language, in the sense of a quotidian American speech, like Ginsberg, Creeley, Diane diPrima, and among older poets, Williams, Pound, H.D., Marianne Moore." She also read Whitman and Hart Crane. Later on, in Latin America, she discovered the work of "César Vallejo, which had a great impact on me. And also the poetry of Sor Juana Inés de la Cruz." Of the poets of her generation, in the United States and Latin America, "there are many I love and who continue to offer me so much: Adrienne Rich, Joy Harjo, Alice Walker, Roque Dalton, Carlos María Gutiérrez, and the list could go on. But I ought to say as well that in my life there are events that have marked me more than the work of other poets."

Randall's work is a vital part of the current trend in North American poetry in which writing by Indigenous, Latina, Afro-American, and Asian-American women is at the fore. She is included with June Jordan, Audre Lorde, Sandra Cisneros, Michelle Cliff, Janice Gould, Sonia Sánchez, Luci Tapahonso, Gloria Anzaldúa, along with those already mentioned above. Randall particularly admires Adrienne Rich as "undoubtedly the greatest American poet; a Jewish, lesbian woman who was profoundly political with an extraordinary vision and power of language." This, of course, is not to say that there aren't outstanding male poets, "but something particular is happening with women writers. Their expression comes from the force of a deep reuniting with their own memory, which had been crushed for so many centuries."

For Randall everything has an ideological dimension. "Literature is always governed by an ideology, even when it's written by those who say they don't have one." Her work condemns injustice, exploitation and violence, the patriarchal order. The social and the intimate are planes in the same universe, and they are integrated, moving from one to the other naturally. She does not believe in the fall of utopias, in the disintegration of the subject, in the death of poetry. She is a poet of this moment and of a better future. Hers is a struggle for absolute liberty—and she is successful because she has the power of image, which cures any lack or loss, even death.

This anthology offers readers a summary vision of an extraordinary body of work that spans sixty years. By including poems from most of Randall's collections, we are witness to the numerous transformations that make up all of her poetic production: the first tentative experiments with content and form, an incipient feminine subjectivity, the development of a radical political consciousness, a committed revolutionary woman, the awakening of sexual identity, the return home, the process of aging, the relevance of nature and landscape. Margaret Randall, the woman and the writer, cannot be understood without it. This anthology also serves as a tribute to Randall as our mentor, who has taught us to struggle in solidarity with others, to confront intolerance and dogmatism, to open ourselves to new times and places, to strive for a world where life and poetry are one.

Katherine M. Hedeen and Víctor Rodríguez Núñez

The Poet's Annotated Chronology

1936:

December 6, Margaret was born in New York City to Elinor Davidson and John Reinthal.

My parents later changed our surname to Randall. I was the oldest of three living siblings; an older sister, also named Margaret, died shortly after birth. This, and my parent's decision to change their name, have haunted my poetry.

Throughout my infancy, my maternal grandfather sexually abused me while my grandmother looked on. This resulted in a lifelong phobia. I buried the memory, however, and did not retrieve it until many years later, in psychotherapy when I was close to fifty. I now believe this experience may have given me my first understanding of injustice, setting me on a lifelong journey fighting for justice on many fronts. The memory retrieval did not put an end to the phobia, but it did make me stronger and more aware. Over time, I developed the understanding that the invasion of a small country by a larger more powerful one is very like the invasion of a vulnerable body by someone who holds more power. This realization continues to echo in my work.

1941:

The attack on Pearl Harbor took place the day after my fifth birthday. World War II, in the Pacific as well as in Europe, had a great impact on my life, provoking my earliest questions about war. My father enlisted at 36, but remained at Fort Knox, Kentucky, until his discharge, after which he worked on the assembly line at an airplane plant in Tarrytown, New York. Air raid drills. Food rationing. *Bundles for Britain.*

1942:

From the age of six, I knew I wanted to be a writer. I could not learn to read along with my classmates in first grade, so my father tutored me each night the following summer and I made the leap at the beginning of second. But poetry eluded me; throughout my school years, it was badly taught as rote memorization, and I could not relate to Wordsworth, Longfellow, even Poe.

1947:

Our parents moved my brother John, sister Ann and me to New Mexico, where we settled in Albuquerque. A radical cultural change from our previous life in the upper-class mostly white suburb of Scarsdale.

1956:

At a party, someone read "Howl". I was mesmerized. For the first time, a poem grabbed me, changed me. I wanted to know Ginsberg, wrote to him care of his publisher, said I would meet him in San Francisco on such and such a night, made the road trip but of course he didn't show. This marked the moment I knew I wanted to write poetry myself.

1956-57:

I married Sam Jacobs. We bought a Lambretta motor scooter and headed for India. We made it as far as southern Spain, where we lived in Seville for a little over a year. I learned Spanish there. The marriage ended in divorce. My young husband was mentally ill and eventually committed to a hospital. Before our split, he burned all that I had written to that point.

Painter Elaine de Kooning spent two semesters as a visiting professor at the University of New Mexico. We became friends, and she a lifelong mentor. When she returned to New York, I followed.

1958:

In New York City in the late fifties and early sixties, friendships with Abstract Expressionist painters and Beat, Black Mountain and New Image poets were important to my understanding art as the center of my life, and to taking my own craft seriously.

I worked at Spanish Refugee Aid under Nancy Macdonald who became an early mentor. SRA board of directors included Hannah Arendt, Mary McCarthy, Dwight McDonald, and others.

1959:

First self-published book of poems, *Giant of Tears*, with original drawings by New York artists Ronald Bladen, Elaine de Kooning, Al Held, Robert Mallary, and George Sugarman.

1960:

Son Gregory born in October. His father was the poet Joel Oppenheimer. Joel and I, however, did not have an ongoing relationship, and I had Gregory on my own.

1961:

Self-published *Ecstasy Is a Number*, with cover and interior drawings by Elaine de Kooning.

First poems published in little magazines: "Any Little Boy Wanting to be President" in *Liberation* and "St. Margaret Stepping from the Belly of the Dragon" in *The Provincetown Review*. Other poems published in *Nomad*, *White Dove Review*, and *The Outsider*.

First readings at Greenwich Village coffee houses.

I sent some of my poems to William Carlos Williams in Rutherford, New Jersey. Williams invited me to visit, and critiqued and encouraged my poetry. This was critical to my early development.

In late summer, I moved to Mexico City with ten-month-old Gregory. I began frequenting informal poetry evenings at the home of U.S. Beat poet Philip Lamantia. There I met Mexican poet Sergio Mondragón, and together we founded the literary quarterly, *El Corno Emplumado / The Plumed Horn*, publishing some of the best poetry of an era, often bilingually, for the following eight years.

1962:

January: first issue of *El Corno* appears. The journal came out every three months until mid-1969, when the repressive aftermath of the 1968 Mexican Student Movement forced it to cease publication. During its eight-year run, I became acquainted with the work of César Vallejo and other Latin American poets—past and current—as well as with that of poets throughout the world. I began translating from the Spanish. During its life, *El Corno Emplumado* published more than 700 poets and artists. The journal proved an extraordinary poetic education.

Sergio and I were married in February in Tepotzlán. Laurette Sejourné and Ida Rodríguez Prampolini served as witnesses. Laurette and her husband Arnaldo Orfila were important mentors.

1963:

Daughter Sarah born in April.

1964:

Poems of the Glass (Cleveland, Ohio: Renegade Press).

Small Sounds from the Bass Fiddle (Albuquerque: Duende Press). Cover and interior drawings by Bobbie Louise Hawkins.

Reading tour of U.S. with Sergio Mondragón.
Traveled alone to read in Placitas, New Mexico, invited by Robert Creeley.
Daughter Ximena born in June.

1965:

October (Mexico City: El Corno Emplumado Press). With photographs of sculptural collages by Shankishi Tajiri.

1967:

Twenty-Five Stages of My Spine (New Rochelle: Elizabeth Press).

Getting Rid of Blue Plastic (Bombay, India: Dialogue Press).

Water I Slip Into at Night (Mexico City: El Corno Emplumado Press). Cover and drawings by Felipe Ehrenberg.

So Many Rooms Has a House but One Roof (New York: New Rivers Press). Poems written out of the Cuban experience.

January, first trip to Cuba, to attend Encuentro con Rubén Darío hosted by Casa de las Américas. I met Haydée Santamaría, who would become a friend and mentor.

Married to a Mexican, I opted to take out Mexican citizenship. This was a purely economic decision; it made it easier to get a job. I did not wish to relinquish my U.S. citizenship, but when I notified the U.S. Consulate, was told I already had.

In October, Ernesto Che Guevara was assassinated in Bolivia on orders of the CIA. A pivotal moment for those considering ourselves revolutionaries.

Sergio and I divorced.

1968:

January, second trip to Cuba, to attend the Cultural Congress of Havana.

The Mexican Student Movement exploded in July. Initial demands revolved around student autonomy. But farmers and unions soon joined the students, giving the movement added impetus throughout the country. The Mexican government, preparing to host the Summer Olympics on October 12, saw its interests threatened. On October 2, paramilitary and military forces fired into a peaceful demonstration at a place called the Plaza of Three Cultures, or Tlatelolco, killing hundreds. Our Movement was finished. *El Corno Emplumado* had been strong in its support of the students, and I personally had taken part in the struggle. The massacre at Tlatelolco taught me the lengths to which a government would go to preserve power.

I began living with U.S. American poet Robert Cohen.

1969:

Daughter Ana born in March.

At the end of this year I began reading the first feminist texts coming out of the U.S. and western Europe. They had a profound effect on my life and work. Feminism—which I regard as a lens through which to examine power—became a core philosophy.

As the Mexican Student Movement's first anniversary approached, paramilitary operatives showed up at our home, threatening me and taking my passport at gunpoint. I was forced underground, eventually traveling via Prague to Cuba, where I would live for the next 11 years. Robert and I sent the four children on ahead, for their safety and our mobility, catching up with them three months later.

In Cuba a group of young Cuban poets—among them Arturo Arango, Ramón Fernández-Larrea, Alex Fleites, Nancy Morejón, Víctor Rodríguez Núñez, Leonardo Padura, Reina María Rodríguez, and Bladimir Zamora—became friends; some of us held a poetry workshop every Saturday morning on the grounds of the University of Havana. During my 11 years on the Island, I also participated in poetry readings throughout the country, at workplaces, collective farms and schools, experiencing the respect for poetry in a socialist society.

1970:

Invited—along with Ernesto Cardenal, Roque Dalton, Cintio Vitier and Washington Delgado—to judge poetry in Casa de las Américas annual literary contest.

1972:

Part of the Solution (New York: New Directions).

1973:

Parte de la solución (Lima, Peru: Editorial Causachún). Translations by Antonio Benítez, Víctor Casaus, Oscar de los Ríos, Roberto Díaz, Roberto Fernández Retamar, Ambrosio Fornet, Carlos María Gutiérrez, Edwin Reyes, and Exilia Saldaña.

Day's Coming (Los Angeles, CA). Privately printed by friends.

I spent three months in Peru, working on gender issues for the United Nations International Labor Office during the Juan Velasco Alvarado administration.

1974:
With These Hands (Vancouver, B.C.: New Star Books).

In Fall 1974 I was invited to the People's Republic of North Vietnam and traveled there, as well as to the liberated area of Quang Tri just below the 17th parallel. I remained in Vietnam through early 1975—until just three months before the U.S. War in Vietnam ended in April. This trip was extremely important to my life and work.

1975:
Robert Cohen and I separated. I began living with Colombian/Venezuelan poet Antonio Castro; we would be together for four years.

1977:
All My Used Parts, Shackles, Fuel, Tenderness and Stars (Kansas City, MO: New Letters).

1978:
Carlota: Poems and Prose from Havana (Vancouver, B.C.: New Star Books).

We (New York: Smyrna Press). Cover by Judy Janda.

I apprenticed to Cuban photographer Ramón Martínez Grandal and began seriously making pictures.

1980:

I moved to Nicaragua, where I lived for the next three years. For the first of these years, I worked at the newly established Ministry of Culture, under poets Ernesto Cardenal and Daisy Zamora. For the following two, I worked under poet Gioconda Belli at another Sandinista institution. Nicaragua is a nation of poets, and I experienced what it is like to live in a country where poetry is a national pastime.

1984:

I returned to the United States, where I would be forced to wage an almost 5-year battle for reinstatement of citizenship, winning my case in 1989. My reconnection with my homeland put me back in touch with my mother tongue and the desert landscape of the U.S. American Southwest which claims an important place in my work. I also discovered the wealth of women poets, especially women of color, at the forefront of U.S. contemporary poetry.

I married and for a year lived with U.S. poet Floyce Alexander. We divorced.

From 1984 to 1994, I taught writing, literature and women's studies at several U.S. universities, including Trinity College in Hartford, Connecticut; the University of New Mexico in Albuquerque; Macalester College in St. Paul, Minnesota; the University of Delaware and Oberlin College in Ohio.

1985:

About a year after my return to the U.S., I recognized my lesbian identity. This gave me deeper insights into my desire, and had a profound effect on my poetry. My love poetry changed in subtle and not so subtle ways, becoming more deeply authentic and more radical, in that it emerged from a place of rebellion against repression.

1986:

The Coming Home Poems (East Haven, CT: LongRiver Books). Published to benefit the Margaret Randall Legal Defense Fund.

I began living with U.S. artist and teacher Barbara Byers. We have been together for more than 31 years now. In 2013, when marriage equality became legal in a number of states, we were married in New Mexico and New York. Aside from being the love of my life, our relationship supports my creativity in ways I never imagined possible.

1987:

This is About Incest (Ithaca, New York: Firebrand Books).

1988:

Memory Says Yes (Willimantic, CT: Curbstone Press).

1992:

The Old Cedar Bar (Nevada City, CA: Gateways). With drawings by E. J. Gold.

Dancing with the Doe (Albuquerque: West End Press).

1997:

Hunger's Table (Watsonville, CA: Papier-Mâché Press).

1998:

Esto sucede cuando el corazón de una mujer se rompe, poemas 1985–1995 (Madrid, Spain: Hiperión). Translations by Víctor Rodríguez Núñez.

2001:

Coming Up for Air (Santa Fe: Pennywhistle Press). After conflict with publisher, author canceled edition, but some copies were sold.

Where They Left You for Dead / Halfway Home (Berkeley: EdgeWork Books).

2004:

Into Another Time: Grand Canyon Reflections (Albuquerque: West End Press). Cover and interior drawings by Barbara Byers.

Dentro de otro tiempo: reflejos del Gran Cañón (Mexico City: Alforja). Translations by María Vázquez Valdez.

2007:

Stones Witness (Tucson: University of Arizona Press). With 30 full-color photographs by author.

2009:

Their Backs to the Sea (San Antonio: Wings Press). Cover painting by Jane Norling. Black and white photographs by author.

2010:

My Town (San Antonio: Wings Press). Interior photographs from archives and by author.

2011:

As If the Empty Chair / Como si la silla vacía (San Antonio: Wings Press). Spanish translations by Leandro Katz and Diego Guerra.

Ruins (Albuquerque: University of New Mexico Press). Black and white photographs by author.

Something's Wrong with the Cornfields (UK and Boulder, CO: Skylight Press). Cover art and interior drawings by Barbara Byers.

Testigo de piedra (Zacatecas: Ediciones de Medianoche).

2012:

Where Do We Go from Here (San Antonio: Wings Press). Chapbook with 18 full-color photographs by author.

2013:

The Rhizome as a Field of Broken Bones (San Antonio, Texas: Wings Press). Cover art by Rini Price.

Daughter of Lady Jaguar Shark (San Antonio: Wings Press). Chapbook, with photographs by the author.

2014:

About Little Charlie Lindbergh and Other Poems (San Antonio: Wings Press).

Beneath a Trespass of Sorrow (San Antonio: Wings Press). Chapbook with art by Barbara Byers.

2015:

Bodies / Shields (San Antonio: Wings Press). Chapbook with art by Barbara Byers.

La Llorona (Matanzas, Cuba: Vigía Handmade Books).

2016:

*She Becomes Time (*San Antonio: Wings Press).

2017:

The Morning After: Poetry and Prose in a Post-Truth World (San Antonio: Wings Press). Cover by Barbara Byers.

El rizoma como un campo de huesos rotos (Mexico City: Secretaría de Cultura and Mares DeCierto). Translation by María Vázquez Valdez.

My four children and their partners have given me ten grandchildren and two great grandchildren.

I have translated numerous books of poetry from the Spanish, among them: *Let's Go!* by Otto-René Castillo; *These Living Songs / Estos cantos habitados* by 15 young Cuban poets; *Breaking the Silences: Poems by 25 Cuban Women Poets; Clean Slate* by Daisy Zamora (with Elinor Randall); *Only the Road / Solo el camino: Eight Decades of Cuban poetry; trillos precipicios concurrencias / pathways precipices spectators* by Alfredo Zaldívar; *Diapositivas / transparencias* by Laura Ruiz Montes; *Lo que les dijo el licántropo / What the Werewolf Told Them* by Chely Lima; *Contemplación vs. acto / Contemplation vs. Act* by Yanira Marimón; *Otros campos de belleza armada / Other Fields of Armed Beauty* by Reynaldo García Blanco; *The Oval Portrait* edited by Soleida Ríos; and *Las altas horas / The Late Hours* by Teresa Melo. I have also translated considerable bodies of work by César Vallejo, Roberto Fernández Retamar, Roque Dalton, Carlos María Gutiérrez, and Violeta Parra.

Throughout my almost six decades of writing, publishing and reading, I have participated in international poetry festivals, including those in Bisbee, Arizona; Burlington, Vermont; Medellín, Colombia; The Border Book Festival in Mesilla, New Mexico; and the International Poetry Festival in Granada, Nicaragua. I have given hundreds of readings of my work, in venues such as The Poetry Center at San Francisco State University; the Union of Writers and Artists (UNEAC) in Havana, Cuba; St. Mark's Poetry Project in New York City; Casa del Poeta in Mexico City; Naropa University in Boulder, Colorado; City Lights Books in San Francisco, California; Beyond Baroque in Santa Monica, California; Bowery Poetry & Science and Poets House in New York City; and Site Santa Fe in Santa Fe, New Mexico. In October of 2012, I represented U.S. poets at the Second Festival of Languages of the Americas at the National Autonomous University of Mexico in Mexico City; eleven other poets read in Spanish, Gauraní, Quechua, Purépecha, Canadian French, Huichol, Totonaca, Maya, Zapotec, and Portuguese. In 2017 I was awarded the Medal of Literary Merit by Literatura en el Bravo, Ciudad Juárez, México.

In addition to my university stints, I have taught poetry at The Taos Writers Conference in Taos, New Mexico, and at Naropa's Summer Writing Program, among others.

Note: Book titles listed on this time line are poetry collections only. I have published dozens of other books of oral history, essay, memoir and photography.

Acknowledgments

My deep gratitude to Katherine M. Hedeen and Víctor Rodríguez Núñez, for reading almost sixty years of my poetry, making this selection, and writing the perceptive prologue. My gratitude, as well, for their friendship.

The generosity of Sabrina Coryell, Paul Lauter, Jane Norling and Tinke Ritmeester helped make this the elegant edition it is. Thank you.

And thank you, Bryce Milligan, for another beautiful book.

FROM

Giant of Tears

(New York: Tejon Press, 1959)

Tradition

Something like a great event is shackled to my foot
Curbstone scrapings help a little, not much
I can't seem to find it,
Where did I put it last?
But it comforts me!

A marvelous gift was given to me by many people:
My heritage, a ritual of tradition –
Where may I throw that package?
So it will not live.

Kindness is a virtue – I don't want to dirty my friends
Give me a place to put my parcel
So no one will find it;
It keeps itself clean.

The length of a life to break those rotten strings,
To obliterate those musty labels and
I keep running across them
In my sleep.

Ah, to vomit every bit of all the source of it
While I can still feel the retching!
Where was that idea?
I've forgotten.

Number 5

for Elaine

Here we can listen
to nightfall
and blow in
the ears of
sunsets
while the
earth
staggers
through
an open
door.

Of Sevilla Now as It Is

Very thin stand the orange trees
Very thin in their half light, young
holding green baskets of orange fruit
away from the grey and the white

                    And they wash their city in white!
                    And they wash their city in powder
of unstained light glaring back at the sun,
spanning away from the grey stone,   cold
                                                            old
                                                            mocking
the center at fine height, heavy bullock
weighting and crowning the top

                    And the white houses
spanning away and away
away and away from the grey

Ole, ole, ole...
¡Venga mi alma, venga! ¡Venga la madrugada!

And the orange trees stand proud
in their rows of even space and height,
stand closed in the will of the churchyard,
but they follow the houses too – follow
the white rows and toss their orange balls
at the new white space

Never a plumb line straight in the
city of cold white heat!

Never a smiling symmetry as women
of purple grief carry their children high and
the gypsy girl dances a passionate truth while
her brother sells the man his own watch
for fifty pesetas

Ole, ole ole...
¡Venga mi alma, venga! ¡Venga la madrugada!

I saw the parade of Moorish Guard when they
made Morocco free, and they held straight standards
from those Andalusian mounts but
　　　　　　　　it all changed, it all changed,
and the cardinal was fat, fat
a silken gut as he smiled and
returned the sign of the goose-steppers
　　　　　　　　Were they wearing German helmets
　　　　　　　　as well?

Ole, ole ole...
¡Venga mi alma, venga! ¡Venga la madrugada!

Madrugada of early morning, silent as
penitentes stumble beneath their crosses
in ceaseless processions
　　　　　　　　Holy week candles in
flickering pairs, crawling the narrow streets,
pushing their way of gold and silver while
the fat priests empty the poor boxes
into their clumsy robes and the tambourines
wail the shadow light from Triana

The smells are sometimes– always
and it's always the olives, that olive oil
laying a heavy vapor over the city of slim

young trees, the trees with their odorous strength
                    Flowers a dusty pollen
wrapping the Plaza Nueva in April air

                    And the olives...

Blood sausage running intestine long from
behind the bull ring to the stalls in
the Puerta de Carne

                    And the olives...

Strong incense from grey arches
heavy lightly out in the streets,
the fish stands and the wine and
urine fresh against white walls

                    And the orange trees,
                    And always the olives

Ole, ole ole...
¡Venga mi alma, venga! ¡Venga la madrugada!

And I look at the trees in their straightness,
olives a full potion heavy and smooth,
And I see the white and the grey
And I catch the carnations that fall from
                    the passing Virgin,
Music that crowds about me–

The tone is like my tone at this moment
                    But I am of a different place

Am I also of a different sense?

Wish

Let me the look
of an angel
so I may
work my
wicked stint
in peace!

FROM

Ecstasy Is a Number

(New York: Orion Press, 1961)

Ecstasy Is a Number

for Jack

All is Number. Number is in all.
Number is in the individual.
Ecstasy is a Number.
—Charles Baudelaire, *Squibs*

tremor tempo our
own voice and
catwalk descending
descended half-hypnotic
midday racing just
behind, half out-swung
and colorless, dizzy
metered limp balance
loose-knit of sense and
summer, wake of total
recall (there is endless
substance, soft soft)
stroking the brain-sharp
vision, stroking stroking
the brain, stroking from
pits of black laughter, idly
playing with the pieces (is it
still raining?) dying
in the light.

The Third Week

the joy of you first baby and
you've won every battle already
making my life a shambles anxious
maternal ignorance and primitive awe

how the beginning creeps in to
stay and the blotting out of each
earlier day in total mad submersion
crumbling fitful staggering up again

those wild eyes not even seeing yet
and knowing the only real comfort of
contact the heat and cold of senses
side by side with wrath of urge

hysteric cry I hear the scream
within myself as well and think I'm
nothing they should come to take
me away I can't I can't I can't

but you are planted in a great
emptiness with strong love and
glad for it, glad for love and
I much more than glad.

Eating the Snow

for Alan

coming from a quivering loneliness
not yet solid or immune
and having to do with sparrows
staying the winter and eating the
snow for water and eating the
snow for water, and eating the snow

staying the winter and eating the snow
it becomes nor heavy nor soft
but sodden with wanting, sodden
in knowing that your space and my space
have happened somewhere apart

somewhere apart that other longing
whistles a wakeful song a charging
of memory splitting this instant to
scattered reminders – again there
are thoughts of the sparrows, a triumph

a triumph in that slow factual
certainty. My child's need puts
me here and my need of you is
an ache, for my child is here.

FROM

Poems of the Glass

(Cleveland: Renegade Press, 1964)

This Is the Way We Say Go

the sky turns
grey tonight
earlier earlier it

has faded
out of sight

a bobbing earth, bobbing
I say
no longer jumps

events have numbed us
spin uneasily,
no numbers

can define
this century the
spell is

settling the
roses grow
from human skin

pulled tight
across the time
of wonder, all

is still, touch me
your fingers
slowly, slowly

let us move.

FROM

Small Sounds from the Bass Fiddle

(Albuquerque: Duende Press, 1964)

Small Sounds from the Bass Fiddle

composing again
from what stands about me
: a fish with black eyes
the painted rooster from my love

letters, sounds of water
trollies dancing through my head
and the way the air hangs
between seasons
there to be breathed
or battled

our son   : his sight
the way we touch each other
the images which speak or sing
and coming to them, using them
lean them to what we need to say
rarely wondering at meaning,
importance, logic and
the learned vestiges

his hand passing over me
in the night
as i curl back
from changing the baby
is much a different hand
than placed the ring
: warmer, grained with
the time we've made,
hold, will hold completely round

the black-eyed fish the rooster
are animate life
: part of what we hold,
see, speak of daily
/it forms itself in lines
and makes a poem/ the meaning
: lost
devoured
evident.

There Is Something for You To Do

through your arm's arc i see the world
turning weight on its left elbow
looking back at us
wondering as we

honey and sesame seeds align
a watery perception
leading its prayers behind
another time
beginning

in your limb's roots i feel the pull
the other summers
collapse and die
the other years recede

there is something here for you to do
something grand, tall
across your chest
the maggot soldiers march

below the window, door to another plane
our son is laughing
inside me
another seed is growing

there is something here for you to do
the numbers arrange themselves
in your open hand

if you turn every card in the tarot
upside down

work your cabala
for every given day
study them all

you will not see beyond that laughter
you cannot count the answers
they will come too fast.

Definition

–felt in the body/ not seated in the mind– of the thing AS A SENSE OF INSTANT. situation in space-time. unconscious for which 'stream of consciousness' is too conscious. the masters used : Pound, Williams, Olson and those before, must be absorbed/digested/discarded in one piece.

we are beyond the form and of it. it must be as the bone structure in the human body, as irreplaceable and as invisible. the poem itself reduced to the communication of its structure-sense-picture. the picture plane worked inside out.

and the application beyond : a retrieving of 'social poetry' *not* in the political/societal sense but in the sense that we are all the living extension of the word/phrase/idea. that which has no beginning and no end. if the poem is life the life is poem the child is wise the time is now. the touching of hands extends horizontally, does not come from above.

the 'talk of poetry' comes goes comes goes, leaves us with nothing but words, aversions, avoidance of center : intellectualization, the making of 'academy'.
　　　　　　　　　　　　　the poem, the word, the eye, the touch – compounded in a fraction of placement : as the child puts his face close to the floor, traces with his finger, the break between plane and plane, looks up, smiles, goes back to it...
　　　　　　　　　　　　　the poem : nothing more or less than our awareness of that encounter, our gift to give it out

FROM

October

(Mexico City: El Corno Emplumado, 1965)

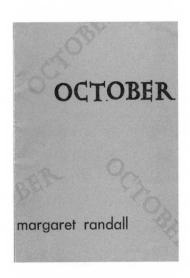

To Answer Your Question

1

i am beneath. flat. round but flat.
what comes
comes from above
with all its possibilities
comes from above
into
in-
to

i am beneath.

2

i am open. wanting.
to be filled.

again.

3

i have joined hands. a rite.
but when the baby comes
burns
climbs, bursts
through
forward, when that moment
frees itself from me
i to it

the rite renewed but otherwise
three times has come to me
will never come again. the knowing that

will never leave.

4

the pale side of the sun
burns itself in shadow.

5

how it feels
not what it's like but
how it feels to be woman
                           when you asked me that
the faces crawled back behind their eyes the
whole circle split again and again
i am looking
at the moon looking
for my reflection there
where it should be
in vain i am searching
the lights and darknesses
believing

i should find myself
in that craterous mirror.

the symbols too easy
their author only a student
was never pulled loose

from the side of man, was never
cut out bounced back
sucked up
cut sucked bounced pulled
that tells some of it tells something
of winter and curtains.

winter and curtains, seasons and place
where sitting still
the female moves inside the skin
dances between bone and tendon
lets a sea unanswered from her eyes
says yes and no
                no and yes
interchangeably.

6

marks to be found
on the pale side of the sun.

These Movements Making Dance

for Judith and Miguel Donoso Pareja

1

in the morning in the morning
                              verily
that word, the sound of it like a river
a small stream over rocks, small rocks and
what happens in being small, being
much smaller
that what so easily is taken in is
grown and handable

what i touch now fights back, being
that time of life for me.

2

in the picture ten buddhist monks
walk toward the camera. away from
the temple. and crazy planes of
ornate grays behind, the monks'
red drapery robes, their small bags, all
they possess not an inch of hair twenty sandals
moving along at bottom. this is a photograph, this

is real. the faces seem soft but
are they, are they the same do they cover
the same trance the same conviction the
very same expression, movement, dance,
towards what place, or

breaking different their dance, a
necessary question. a
moving window.

3

from the day from the day
                              the night comes
cutting out words, erasing them, making of them
their own shadow, sullen afterbirth
invented. and even this,
and even this unripe or
passed its moment, precision
counting for so much. the foot and finger
forward. so much.
responsibility
moving away from the hand, moving
beyond the crutch of touch, the
scar of pride sealed off, away, immediate
and disperse world
                              breaking
so many fractures, facets. too many.

4

a matter of relating tensions, connecting
places, songs, giving up
the dance
         out
pleasing the continuous
line, never dying.

if i were a painter i would

paint in great coats of black, the canvas,
shining and dripping, a
never drying pigment
glossed across interminable space
coating in black also myself, also
my own body. draped in red but painted black.

5

and this line too, moving in space
is dance. kept inside
its own circumstances, bent
by its own history, pushing a
sign to move with.
this, what we call dance. each space
united or departed
from father, from son. gives off
as inheritance bringing us
to term, cuts our direction,
tries us out.

here we create a stage, a platform
of sorts, put sets, the props with which
we move
from which we turn, curtains
to conceal
our change of scene, remove our days
one from another.

6

this dance. this sequel
our limbs penciling in air

the throat's intention. this making separate
what is whole
and making whole what by another voice
is time.

Places

1

when the sun goes out the
water eases, marks of erosion
on the face neck hands when
the air comes thin and needed, not
enough of it to hold in the lungs
not enough of any piece place, settling
of time through
tired filters
when these common fillings
become used, gray, strained to
touch and senses

long sinews holding to
chronic posture, eyes bleeding
behind the porous skull, eyes
of tinsel paper on the white sugar
cranium
        old as the dia de muertos
dead as repeated signs repeated
gesture, wheel turning with no hand
hand on a wheel that is not there

enough that the sinews
do not break, enough that
the wheel turns invisible, continues
in that instant big as a man, man
big as a world, world big as
a meaning
: small as a thumbprint
on the moving line...

2

it is the way you see
the circle, moving, what
you choose to call
                        from what books
how loose or tight, to what
place coming
the blame, ingredients
propped up and fitted together
one into another, one over
or under another
can it be zodiac or metric table
sun setting rising heating, tearoom
with every object there
                        different
being in itself a new dimension, broken,
a cup a leaf a new
or old concern. the mask removed
replaced

in history another circle
resettled, timed to new ears
movement
chosen by chance stroke the
big clock
            was stopped
will never move again will never
advance digit by digit
close over
another stroke separate
another division in our ears
new ingredients, circles

with new names
coming at eye level
onto the stage.

The Difference

these still earth gods
chamulas huixtecos zinacatecos
rub their bare legs
with the oil of jungle nuts, walk

the chiapaneco mountains
those legs glistening, shining
in strong sun, cutting black
through fifty kinds of green.

those great wide faces
close to me in the market of
san cristobal de las casas, eye to eye
stand still before the same

dried shrimp or mountain fruit
look at me
and i return the same cold unmoving eyes
caught for one weight of time, one

question. the old jews
still moving in my past, move
today, have never stopped. this man
stands still, he

does not move at all as
his long black oiled olympic legs
walk fast through these hills
he does not move at all

as he looks down his mayan nose
at me and i move out
in all ways, on all waves,
asking...

Margaret, ca. 1940, at home in Scarsdale, New York.
Family photograph.

Margaret, late 1950s, in Albuquerque, New Mexico.
Photograph by Sam Jacobs.

Margaret, ca. 1957, New York City.
Photograph by Eddie Johnson

Margaret in Havana, 1970, signing copies of *Las Mujeres*.

Left to right around the table: Margaret, Rodolfo Walsh,
Laurette Séjourné, Silvia Gil, Alfredo Guevara, Manuel Galich,
Haydée Santamaría, Raul Roa, and others,
at Casa de las Américas, Havana, 1970.

FROM

25 Stages of My Spine

(New Rochelle, NY: The Elizabeth Press, 1967)

25 stages
of my spine

Margaret Randall

The Elizabeth Press
New Rochelle, N.Y.

7

and that, too...

the daily press instructed
makes a case for johnson's trip
big daddy
from the north
he stretches his hand in clenched fist
the workers

get the day off are paid
in truckloads
they come waving little flags
through wine and caviar the american ambassador
plays his trombone
and ladybird sings guadalajara

o guadalajara
memories of honeymoon
and little mexican children
taught once by the big man
in texas
where mexicans and dogs are not let in
to certain places
ranchstyle houses oil wells or
telephone booths
his hand on the phone

a private line
his hand on the phone the busy signal says
the line is dead

13

the dream, in space...

i lie down
on that corn altar
growing out of my eyes the ears
from between the toes of my feet
and hands
the corn
as instrument
feelers jumping to a static call
from my hands from the stages of my spine

the knobs bent
coiled
corn   a rope   that altar
husks ripening as hearts
offered up
cut out and offered up
only

the altar remains
and i from years
laid out on it

25

sergio...

and to say i love you
like flowerpots
the filling stands aside
is only what covers what goes
around it

words a blanket
or roof
walls already mossing
better to say

come
be with me here
run your feet in time with mine
my own with yours
come
sit on this honeycomb

of firelight
and fists
corners and waves of loose warm air
catching us
putting us where
our own reflection

speaks to us

FROM

Water I Slip Into at Night

(Mexico City: El Corno Emplumado, 1967)

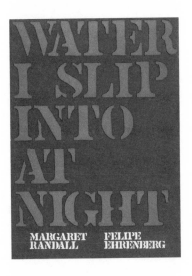

Poem for my Thirtieth Year

1

i would still be there
with my hands before me
stretched out, waiting,
if i were not here

holding what
left to me of that dream
sticks to my tongue
like unbaked seeds, bitter,

herbs among themselves
i rest only between going there
and being here where i am
undressed

2

to have set this thing up, come out
any other way would have been
a lie. a history

only the crumbs, reverse impression, pain
around the edges
empty spaces where the cloth's been
cut away, how to

measure or construct, it builds
what from its entrance connects it
a way out

3

oh,
it's all right now it's all right i understand
finally in mouth, arms, in the constant sea that cuts
my legs, water

i slip into at night
or barely raised very white of the day that spreads out
before me

A Poem for March

if i kneel down over that map
take the thing from above
with my hands
will point to those roads going
somewhere
to be more definite, say   :that line
means coming through, somehow,
the time you stood hand in hand, next to,
me having the baby
and then another
that line
not head or heart but old flowers
too heavy too cold

to be thrown away.
if you scream at me
               ha!
               you're a *great* writer
               try being a mother
               for a change
and i come back
               get out   get out   get *out*!

our arms drawing together
joints speaking
voices   fingers   hair
the touching

the touching and the map spreads out
involves

decoding our names
the names of our children

i kneel down over that

The Playback

for Connie Boyd

in the silence in the black silence
of this room
it is later than the soles of my feet can find
as they move out
breaking in darkness feeling along the wall
turning a corner, opening

a door that moves towards my fingers, fist
i go in
sit down in the full black of this room
which is mine
late and humid, thick
about the chords my shoulders make
skin of my throat, neck,

because it is my room my poem in the air

pictures, ears i would talk to close about me
elements put to be object, things
familiar in head but covered here in darkness
because this is mine

i shut the door erase these recent days
and lean against a wall a month ago
where someone spoke

i didn't quite hear the end of that story
my hands still waiting for the words to fall
to catch them

The Happening

for Thomas Merton

so long a time feeling less
and acting more on that
to bring it up, cover

the parties where my presence a necessity
the sound of my own voice to my own ears
and the parties where my absence needed me

removed
in another room, listening
(how well things are going without me)
all that time

reaching behind me, hands clasped, wilting
the loud voice
on and on the music of pretext
i am climbing out of my own mind
stepping

out of that place like a skirt
it drops to the floor, needing time
to walk with this new image
reduced to light
repeat.   the place,
you come to that, arrive
or grow up

                    explanation not the same
                    as take with your hands

it is part of you, somewhere,
:stand,
there on that great grassy meadow
with your lever tip the world

over

Using the Same Words

i wanted to tell you
everything
the first places the long times made of silence
the parks
trees crowded together the light between them
disappearing, going out like old sirens, the air
after being broken
where the streets come together
i wanted to tell you stroking and stroking my hair
you listened

i wanted to talk about men repetition
the uncontrollable tremor between the legs
and children the long taking leave
begun in ecstasy, put your hand here,
i wanted to say places dates names pieces of mirror
and stencils of history
knowing you heard beneath the words
the other music running along inside
you listened

i said
surrounded by water an island
now
these words have gone back
recovered original form
                  tense
                      place
the absolute center.

if i ate nothing for five days it was because air
revolution the earth beyond and under my feet

i needed nothing but that.
god knows if you understood
you listened.

Authority, or the Autopsy of Love

for Rita Siegel

when they had me
six years
then it was just a preying mantis
stained on the seat of my blue jeans
                what we called them then
and the furtive wash
in the bathroom my hands remembered
the five dollar fine
a conversation turned to jail
in my head.   authority

made accident a possibility hard put
the hands remembering, washed,
erased where i sat down already

they had me in twenty five years later
american embassy mexico city
no questions but certain knowledge
plans bigger than either, the safety belt
tight
throttled that same authority it's a fear
born

bred and built-in
comes with a do-it-yourself
ointment for the nervous rash
garbage to sit in while you wait.

afterwards
always afterwards reason separates the pieces

claims
the lock on the door came in your christmas stocking
can't keep out or let in
that's for the dark blue or berry red
come to take you by the hand

when they had me in love
it was something else till it ended
or the shadow fell against all gravity and now
you have it in both hands
by the pins and bolts it is closed between fingers
and does not seem to matter that you read

:made in china
smuggled out through hong kong

and counterfeit.

You Turn a Corner and

for Roberto Fernández Retamar and Adelaida de Juan

i too remember the place
when the place was not a corner, not easily
angles
or something more abstract
                              that
making it knowable, come
follow me you have seen it the eye going out
along the top of a wall
a garden you know on the other side
perfectly combed
or not, a place to sit down in

that is how you count backwards, put yourself
again in that place
able to take in your fingers, separate,
your parents are going to capetown
now
they have no reason not to
                              no reason
to say
on a matter of principle
i will make sacrifice, when it isn't,
not even that

if born in the clean of things it's the scum
that draws, attracts,
always comes to the tongue and so you go
to bronx or the lower east side
sit on the stoop
                    stain

the same hand and the hand remains
the same
a balance
ice in your mouth, warm blood
between your legs

it's a good place does not
charge too much, tells no tales
behind you
you are gone into godhead and powered grace
what's not yours
                              you're sold
under the counter or through the mail
nothing
is felt, the pain
killed before it came,
every pore protected
but sudden the place becomes the corner
is joined
of itself is met
on a wild death, the terrible cries don't stop
in your ears
in your mouth you taste the words
                              alive
in you wanting to change them make them more plain
hide them from breath they blow
on the water all the new nets
that sing

i am gone now but that place
is cut in me
crazy the words that lose their nights and days
change
before me along the same wall in the garden, yes,

you remember
                she who taught me this
:when i knew i was going to die i said
now i will learn to die well
and when i lived i will know how to live,
my hands that are

my brothers

The Dead Phoenix

for Anna and Agustí Bartra

tonight a wishbone cracks in my throat
the sun
cursed into blackness, tonight
i would cry
          gravel and blood harpoons
on my country, still my country
refusing to let you go tho the papers
changed hands
tho circumstance found me
here or there or fat or aging
still
you sit on my eyes a sick and spreading fruit
stinking through rotten skin
with hands with long green arms
great fungus on the world
oh tonight i would cut your wrists a terrible love
between my legs
i would drain you and fill your veins
embalming thirty years of tender faith that act
and watch you sink and know
no god you trust

FROM

So Many Rooms
Has a House
but One Roof

(Massachusetts: New Rivers Press, 1968)

1

the grey interior comes alive
and burns, it is
a natural quickening
what you see with the eye, touch

the hand runs over it
picks up, the fingers ache or curl
under
(i remember not being able to sleep, the moon
crying in my mouth, half open, the current
jolting and jolting our bodies)

this landscape hurts
as it shows me everything is real, everything
equal to its own weight
to touch it touches off the pain inside
: those who stay at home have never left
but those who go do not arrive
                          only here

it is different, this circle too
is fire, burns,
makes the measured breath
impossible.

oh, it is all one, together, it is all divided, open,
never to be repeated, always to be eaten,
swallowed whole.

3

i have held off in all things, response
being slow in me
                        to come, lift
its head
yes, i have waited

against the movement of my hands
while filling space with dancing feet
wise shoulders, cocky eye and ears
with premature death in them.

i have been child,
lover, wife, mother
even aged and all the roles converging
playing upon themselves
in me

left open
            salty
                    half, or
overdrawn in pieces
being
all of them and never only one.

at thirty i go unwilling into girdles, painful
coming whole.

5

in that place moncada, the farm house
where they met the night before
took an old couple to carnival or the party
for a fifteen year old girl

the barracks the photos the uniforms
heavy with blood, they were
crazy
and clean, one hundred and forty

men against moloch
against all it is necessary
to be against
and more than half suffered the fat hand
there at moncada, suffered

and died.
the other half grew six years

        so many rooms has a house but one roof

labored in birth, came through
the sun wiping blood from its eyes
stretching
its wide mouth in song.

11

at the level of arches, columns
framed in mahogany pieces of sky
a gull floats
moves his wide wings towards poets
we

are sitting with cut grass, the colors
of sea
these blues and greens invade, belong
to us

as once belonged to dupont
or (as i prefer to think)
never belonged but built by him
preparing for a change of colors he refused
could not have held in hand

or eye.

dupont built this fortress
of a house
a wide gull floats beside the cupola
dupont prepared the golf course
where egrets and wild hens nest

and poets walk. we sit, it is
different now
dupont was mason, paid the help, drank
daiqueries
but the gull turned, the change came

brute

and sure
dupont fled this peninsula and died
and poets sit, keep company
with this gull
stayed with revolution on his wing.

12

the eight year old profile
says
here, i will show you
and it's not even eight if you count

the invasion, cyclone in 63
having to invent, everything, subversion
and blockade.

the profile of eight years
shows articulate lips, eyes with music in them
strong teeth
settles over the island like

the words of a poem
catching up with themselves.

FROM

With Our Hands

(Vancouver, B.C.: New Star Books, 1974)

Exile

A comrade also away from his country said
"for a revolutionary there's no such thing as exile"
and I believe him
with my head
but my body aches for that place
where I will fumble, fall and stand with my sisters and brothers
learn on terrain I have in my bones and boots, take my place
in that people's army
looking to find our tribe
where X is organizing, my sister's waking up,
my father still thinks it can change inside
(because its been sixty years of damage for him)
I have three nieces and nephews I've never met
and that Greyhound bus line Chicago one a.m. looms behind my
eyes
just because it was my last look
                              touch, feel...

Whenever I sit down to write about women
which is supposed to be my job
the first draft
is nowhere the economic base or socialism undercutting the reason,
reserve labor force or any of the rest of it,
it's
lobotomy as the final solution to the woman problem
"successful operation: signs of lessening depression,
even though she was released to go shopping
and committed suicide"
it's "after all those years in the joint
I was finally the one in the black leather jacket"
it's eyes and mouths ogling me down the street
in this transitional society

or the inevitability
of my own woman's madness long hot stove four kids
and a second draft
             and a third...

All I can say today about my children
is that every day my off-key shrieks are further clotted
by deep knowledge
the pain of love that sags or can't take a deep breath,
impatient rage, striking wild
against mistaken targets...anger turned out against your bellowing
in shame at my own high-pitched musical chairs.
In spite of it all I see them
growing up revolutionaries,
teaching us
teaching us
leaving as revolutionaries, out of my line of fire,
that great people's war in their eyes
                    in their hearts...

What can I say about you
is that I don't want to be ashamed
I don't want to fall over with that heavy weight,
sometimes I answer 1955 and it's 1972
but sometimes you're also 1955 though that's ten years old for you
and in weakness I fall into my own closeup ancient history
competition
    and fear.
At the same time
dealing with a battlefield of growth,
I weave a whole new circle because "you wanted to be alone"
or you come home shaking with tension and I'm in the middle
of a raging sentence.
Closeness that keeps on burning beyond itself.
I love you all over the books and grasses.

Learning to see every day with new eyes, the circle widens,
what we've lived together
pushing that forward

open ended...

This is just a cyclical explosion.
The pressure's building up (and I wanted to write a poem)
The last time I wrote like this
was when they killed my brothers at Attica
and I wrote "I am Attica"
and wondered for months: am I? I wasn't there, my gut was there
but I'm here
looking out to sea
measuring out rice
standing guard on the block just before the hot sun comes up
or at my work place, emulation, production,
to the Plaza with Fidel.

Far from my sisters, another culture,
but the same revolution. Crazy Horse and Comandante Che Guevara.

July, 1972

The Fight

My head explodes with the tears that keep coming and coming
beyond all my socialized vows to disown them. Forever.
I don't want to cry in front of you anymore. I WON'T.
but I do.
Over and over again. Humiliating myself
all over my face to you.
You need space and I make you pay for it.
(The bitterest taste of your own medicine.)
So then I don't make you pay. But where is that space?
Suddenly you decide I should share it.
YOUR decision, understand,
ON YOUR TERMS. As long as it's your decision.
Pull the strings.
Pull the strings.
Don't pull my strings anymore.
They can't be pulled.
They don't work.
I don't want you pulling my strings anymore, goddammit,
and I don't want you tangling them either,
matting them with big words to cover lies. Aghast. Purple.
If trying to make me think I'm crazy is your new tactic
it won't work.
My head is a glass ball or a clenched fist
with blood tricking between the fingers
and Annie's soft cheeks beneath each finger nail.
This anguish doesn't even stand up
in the words of conventional warfare.
The hair on my chin is my revolutionary internationalism
aching to go home and struggling to build.
My human body sags with the weight of your love
and moves with the strength of your love

but if you keep pushing me with your inherited billy club
you won't find me in the trench next time

after the fight:

The above was written with hammers pounding
and sickles scraping out the inside of my skull.
The classic fight.
How to reach bottom, paint for you
in clear letters, no rhetoric,
the wildness of my anger?
There is an immense difference between the confusion you want to
    put on me
and the real woman's madness of my teeth. I am dead in life
from the silences we let grow and prosper in our struggle.
I want the struggle of our struggle, just that.
Stand up sit down and listen. Anyway
here's my demilitarized zone: craters and work.

February, 1973

FROM

Carlota: Prose and Poems from Havana

(Vancouver, B.C.: New Star Books, 1978)

Bottlecaps Are Everywhere

The idea was to eliminate every unnatural sign, every synthetic. The accumulative conglomerate: Civilization. Out of the range of my vision went the black telephone wires strung from post to post, small birds sitting confidently on them. Away with the asphalt of the highway, the intrusion of billboards. Even the smallest remnant: a rock chipped by human tools, a tire tread in the heavy sand, a wisp of cloth snagged on a branch, a crushed beer can, bottlecap or crumpled piece of paper. Who drank the beer? What did the paper say? My eye traveled slowly, making sure.

I was fifteen, sixteen then. Walking away from the highway I would follow the protrusions and hollows, rises and falls of a Geological Survey map. Finding the spot. The spot where twentieth century fell away and I would move myself to that space in time where this land was virgin, untouched, original. A measure of the conqueror in me? I closed my eyes and imagined I was riding with Coronado or Cortez, riding this open country, discovering the unknown. But I also imagined —and much more often— that I *lived* in this place before it had been desecrated by the machine, the "white man," a ruling class, property, the idea that land air sun water and work do not belong to everyone who uses them but to one group of humans exploiting another.

Sometimes I would strip beneath the sun, curl up or extend my naked body over a warm flat rock and just look into the sky for hours. For centuries. If I had known then what I know now! But in a sense, in the very amorphous nature of my ramblings, I learned. I learned about space, about time. I learned about patience and about the power of the earth, contempt, peace, temperature, size, pride, color and numbers.

Desert nights are cold. Hard. The earth still cool into midday. Not until hours past noon does the sun succeed in warming the immense body responding to it. Sand warms then. Trees stretch. Tiny piñon nuts fall at the gentlest touch of branches. Arroyo beds glisten in their mineral deposits: rust, green, yellow. Waterless. Colors are pale and dusty. Vegetation on the desert is survival of the fittest, of the toughest, of that which needs the least moisture, the least warmth, the least care. Tenderness is not a quality there. The flat shale beneath my body breathed slowly to my need.

Why did I want to blot out my life and time, turn my face backwards, experience the loss of centuries, the gain of volume, a strength in this certain knowledge –fictitious and temporal– in my path? Once I slept all night alongside the worn and eroded tombstones of a ghost town long ago abandoned. Tejón. Once I walked until dusk along the high ridge of the river gorge –the midland Río Grande– and sought shelter for the night in the home of an old Scotsman, his one-armed Indian wife and their eleven dogs.

The sand was always familiar beneath my feet. The land belonged to anyone who wanted it, to anyone who needed it. But that was all in my head. The land really belonged to the Anderson-Clayton Company, to the US military bases where the improved atomic bombs were being made –even then– to a crooked Indian Commission, to the rapists of soil, the hang-bellied cattleman and a gluttonous government that spoke for, but not in the name of, a people. The land had been Mexico. It had been Indian land. Finding out was part of growing up.

Nineteen-fifty-two on the New Mexican desert: the oppressors finally relinquished their ban on liquor for injuns and the sand received a lesser strewing of bodies fallen out before their "natural" end, the death-from-exposure of the Indian who had to drink up beyond the Law, before Light, outside Time forever. They had made the bomb too behind those fences at Los Alamos, and haunted scientists became the focal point: debates, guilt, necessity, "our" politics. Was it really ours? Somehow...

Senator Joe pulled a curtain of silence over our heads and our memories collapsed for a while under the Madison Avenue version of our lives. It wasn't the US government that developed that bomb, that built it, that dropped it finally on cities of "yellow men." It was −even years later− the pilot who went mad and wrote begging for understanding, the mental anguish of a single human being, science with or without the people, formulas for complacency. But not to last forever.

On the desert there are high power lines, towers that loom in any foreground, die in any direction. Distance. Tracks of tires of all sizes criss-cross their own history again and again and again. Crushed beer cans are everywhere. Bottlecaps are everywhere. We have learned who drinks the beer, who flicks the caps from a passing car. Civilization is in the eye of the beholder. Nineteen-fifty-two has become 1962 and 1972 and 1976. Korea has become Vietnam, and now Angola. The Indians have gone back to Wounded Knee. Cortez keeps riding, and the last frontier is 360 degrees around the globe.

Motherhood

Across my childhood America
there were statues of The Pioneer Mother
I think they must have been almost identical
in every town over 30,000
my adolescent 1950s
remembering my Albuquerque New Mexico
and in the cities they were especially hidden
that slight embarrassment
in some small park or nondescript square
well away from the pulsing downtown
the thriving lakeside or stadium
you know, neither shantytown nor business district,
just there

The forward leaning woman with her bonnet
and the young child in her arms
the child was probably a son
long pioneer skirt swirling stone about her ankles
was she 20, 30, or 40?
A stone basket on her arm or a stone bundle
the hands were large
work hands, hands that built a nation
all while keeping in a suitable background
and the grey stone eyes slightly raised
fixed on something way off there
called god or hope or maybe just the next day

I used to want to stand and look at that woman
for hours.
I never did.
My parents dispensed with it as bad sculpture.
In our history books the pioneer mother

the pioneer woman was flat page after flat page
she came to America to the new land
in a sailing vessel salt pork and sloping decks
riding the waves.
If she lived she was already a heroine,
the rest was a collection of phrases repeated
and we repeated them dutifully:
she-worked-the-land-with-her-man-
reared-her-children-fought-off-savage-indians-
was-god-fearing-man-fearing-and-good,
and those who weren't
were not in the books

It was years before I chipped that picture away
cleaned it with the help of sisters
found the Indian woman beneath the education
they put on us,
understood the women who came to buy their freedom
and remained enslaved,
understood the women who asked questions
who weren't in the books
the Iroquois council women
or General Harriet Tubman.
Sojourner whose whole arm
not just her hand
but her arm was centuries of work,
and she stood up and said
Look at this arm of mine...!

This arm of mine!
It's not only the history they took from us,
women of the mills, great textile strikers
erased with a Madison Avenue sweep of the IBM,
the presses keep rolling
and out come the raped showgirls the murdered actresses

what sells
always what sells,
and a million red satin hearts
the valentine box the mother's day card
the flowers the pressed flowers the corsages
a million five-pound boxes
$7.95 or one for every budget
and the mother becomes the $7.95 mother
or the $2.29 mother if that's all you have
and if you don't know how to say it pretty
Hallmark will say it for you
in a thousand different verses where wife rhymes with life
and Sojourner isn't there
not anywhere
and neither are the million Indian women
and the factory girls the machine operators
the cutters the walkers the runners

Deep among the sequins or in the red velvet
the waitress becomes Marilyn Monroe
and Marilyn Monroe becomes Marilyn Monroe to the nth degree
it's not just history, our grandmothers,
the peoples of other lands
and our relationship to them,
it's the exact sciences too
the pure ones
they cut and rearrange for us:
math abstracted from living,
the physics of survival, our chemical components,
the geography of our minds

Studying and imitating those mothers
we worked hard
so our own would be just like one next door
we rejected even her timid unsure gropings

so we could be fully certainly and definitively
just like the girl across the street
no fatter no thinner
identically dressed and scented
talking about the same things
and with the same expectations
the right kiss a hope chest patterned silver
a single strand of pearls
the set diamond the plain gold band
and the white dress that would cover it all,
I mean all the doubts, anything left unsaid,
anything at all that didn't fit in
or grew unwieldy, too large, showed,
came out when it shouldn't. Couldn't.
The right dress the right man the right job (his)
and on to children!
We too
can be, must be
mothers!

Sometimes it didn't work out just that way
like for Patricia
whose mother smiled and smiled and went away one day
went to the hospital
and came back in an empty suitcase
carried by her silent father
who wouldn't say
couldn't say till after it happened
YOUR MOTHER DIED OF CANCER
it was too hard
so of course there were exceptions
and Patricia became her own mother
played the role
cared for and closed her lips
opened her eyes

wide
wished alone and made decisions
approved the new mother finally
and went on her own marked way

Cancer, a mother's disease
in highly developed USA
when it didn't kill it carved a future
indivisible middle class ways and means,
just like the bourgeois heart attack
or working class TB,
eyes turned away, closed words,
like your mother Robert
who developed bravery as a weapon,
or my own whose womanhood
—not motherhood but womanhood—
grappled around itself as a result,
cancer cancer that terrible word
smelling of the society it breeds
and bred by it
to be whispered to be feared
to be held as deadweight and evidence
supplying committees
foundations and research grants
sported by first ladies now
charities and a tabulated madness

For even a mother's madness
is electronically counted
registered and shelved
here comes another may tenth and another
the beauty parlors are filled
there are pills now
science keeps moving ahead
development is a wonderful thing

there are pills that all but stop time
push history back on itself
you stay young forever and ever
and youth is everything–
everything, do you hear, everything?

Not a line not a wrinkle
I've never seen my own mother
with one grey hair on her head,
till the walls fall around you
and you emerge, parchment,
one terrifying final moment
like Shangri-la,
the face that has always been perfect
lifted and smooth
screaming into a web of lines
a matrix, a map
that says years, a lifetime,
the final admission of having lived.

And I think of that Latin American mother
Carmen of the narrow hills
going up and up
the people in weather patched shacks
Carmen of the soft eyes
her hands have worked as hard as any
her son in prison in exile in distance
and the weight of every day
like finding and making
just what holds them together
just what feeds them
just barely, the family,
and I remember her soft smile breaking
the tears coming just once as she said
No. No, let him stay where he is.

I love him but I don't want him back
for here it's just struggle
the fear all the time
prison again
let him stay where freedom is
where his children too will be free

My pelvic bones move apart now
they spread
as I take my own motherhood in my hands
hold it and look at it
talking to this person, this woman,
as if it were me. Yes.
Feel the life creeping back to my flesh
into my bones
my hips widen,
acknowledge Gregory
then Sarah
Ximena of the wise eyes
little Anna
remembering the wet rush of that moment
remembering it in eyes and hands
moving with it, standing up,
this is my own arm,
and then learning, slowly,
that motherhood is never that moment,
giving birth is only the beautiful explosion,
the beginning,
the giving and taking is every day
as what comes from you
grows
and moves away

And you learn to let him go let her go
give and take and give

as the distance widens
and you try to put the real world in that space
the whole struggle
love that's as hard as the stone bonnet
as rough as that heaving sea
as full as the empty suitcase
as common as the red satin heart
as big as the lowell strikers
as strong as her arm

my arm

The Homeland

The homeland
calls out to us in great voices
like the mother to her son when dinner's served
and he's gone in search of something
to adorn the table
—Antonio Castro

The homeland calls
and a new land is born within us
birth
    rebirth
my homeland is America
from the Río Bravo to the Patagonia
my homeland was America north of the great river
is North America still
beyond passport and bourgeois law
my homeland is the courage of Vietnam
the wail of the andean quena
hands that knead the nixtamal
eyes that laugh and cry
the creek where Crazy Horse's heart lies ready
the Trail of Tears
the trail of Sojourner
Sojourner's bare breast and bare arm
Che's shoulder in the wet air of morning
Michaela
Vallejo Vallejo your humerus bones your hunger
the accent hanging from your shoe.
When the fighter stands on the outskirts of his life
turns and waves to the woman
who waves growing smaller and smaller
my homeland is the fighter who leaves

and the woman who stays behind
and when it's the woman who goes
my homeland is also she
who carries both gun and child.
My homeland is green and brown
bright yellow baking earth
my homeland is red blood
and red flags
red
and redder still.
My homeland is the river rising
to bury life and even anguish
those who have nothing and only want something
those who work something not theirs
who work and work
what always belongs to another
and still work and still sing and still fight.
My homeland is the struggle
where it leaps and crawls
where it comes together and moves forward
pushes and is pushed by history
by peoples
my homeland is the people
the mother and her son
the search
and what finally adorns the table.

October 8, 1975

FROM

We

(New York: Smyrna Press, 1978)

Margaret Randall

Ammon the Young

Sometimes I think of you. It's been a long time. I see your lean body aging into some angular perpetual youth, forearms swinging, even tone to the answers, clean blue eyes bringing Southern California, New Mexico, Texas fields, migrations to stay clear of taxes, prison to stay clear of taxes and of war, prison as a way of life: as you wrote we did this and that, we spread the Word and God was a bowl of hot soup on the Bowery, nothing was out of order, God was also a song or the even tone, words spaced between words, a little goes a long way but a long way is never enough. I can pick up the placards held high "I AM AMMON HENNACY: ARREST ME" and the big full peaches, one a day for your visits, my first child hospital ward. Or I can pick out one August protest, sixteen years since the Hiroshima Bomb and sixteen days of protest, the vigil on the Court House steps, the tiny cut limes squeezed over your fasting lips. I can pick out the papers midday on Wall Street, a penny a paper, a penny a smile, a penny a word or not. Always the good word, always the good smile. Always the good long arms and the good blue eyes. Then you went away, you followed the prophets to the valley of salt, Joe Hill not Smith, and married they said, married a woman of nineteen for your angular seventy or eighty years. And later I was there and talked about finding you and looking into those eyes again but only talked about it and never did it and never saw you again. And you died like all strong men finally do, in the stifling migrant barracks in the prison cells and soup kitchens on the Court House steps and on the rails you still want to sweep and hurl.

Nothing Was the Way It Was

You and your mother. No one understands why you don't relate to women or to men either but relate to everyone and write Future and have the best power of analysis of anyone anyone knows. We talk about everything but that. In the Cauto River Valley in the little wooden house halfway between river and lagoon your father brought in a large cheese and your mother plucked the turkey and flattened fried banana slices. You were angry about your books being moved about, nothing was the way it was, one of them had been eaten through by a termite moving from page to page and we tried to laugh about the chosen words. Your mother and father seemed the happiest of couples. Then one day your mother came to the city and we talked again. A year older than me: it's just that we're women... And she began to tell her story of abuse:...jealous of his own sons... why there were years he'd go out for the day with my sewing machine bobbin in his pocket so as how to keep me from sewing he thought I'd make money on the side and spend it, ayyeee...And the tears and the face turned away and then the face towards me, full front, and the exact replica of events, battles, endurance these twenty seven years. I told her I thought the best thing she could do would be this leavetaking, this new beginning, this final avowal to be her own self. And she said she thought she would go and live with you, in Bayamo...You and your mother...You and the Revolution...You and Martí and Céspedes and Rilke in the grass, the careful lines of your childhood poem, the ninety six year old trovador you discovered in Ciego and the day I gave you the pin with Marinello's likeness because you're the only person I know who cried because you weren't there to see the great man when the people bid him goodbye.

Parallel George

It was that day in the car, both of us moving forward, looking straight ahead in the front seat, that the good old days baseball fan mows the lawn when not teaching Canadian Literature father of one and proud look on your face began to crack. It was so good finding you in a parallel space of time, all those years, eleven –wasn't it?– and we could talk about Cuba and Africa and Yugoslavia, women writers and what goes on inside the tightness of the breast. We could talk about your daughter's colored letters and numbers all over the page, all over the bright suburban refrigerator later on that night –exclaiming over the coincidence!– and we could talk about L who had shut himself away and the marriage that isn't good but you accepting that as natural, normal, what's the word? And again the tightness in the breast. Coming together again, after eleven years, there in your northern home I got hooked on an electric typewriter (yours) and stoned on U.S. big prize shows: women exploding across the colored screen, riding the fenders of mile-long buicks, men doing nothing but jumping, jumping, jumping and screaming out numbers. Money! And you said U.S. TV dominates Canadian TV and U.S. radio dominates Canadian radio and what the hell –in that flattest of voices. And that was the thing. What the hell. Moving along like parallel lines but that flatness from your choice: to do nothing but what the skywriting on the underside of your suburban lawn mower prescribes: Canadian Lit and baseball keeping things up for the basement renters, asking occasional questions and driving straight on. Over pancakes we decided it had to do with the untended newsstands: put your quarter in and take a paper. And why don't people take all the papers, I asked or all the quarters? That's just the point, you answered. And we both thought of Mexico, 1964, or anywhere else in the other world where humans devour paper and coins as well as food when they can find it. When I talked about free medical attention in socialist Cuba and you, a Canadian, said you were an adult before you realized that every country didn't have that –natural, normal– assistance, I understood a little more. I mean about Canada not really being an extension of the States, like we were taught. Now we're into the next eleven years and your letters on yellow paper and with a bubble gum wrapper or serious newsclipping inside say I was just thinking about finishing the last novel and now she wants me to paper the den and I was just thinking.

Margaret, 1980, Hartford, Connecticut.
Photograph by Bud Schultz.

FROM

The Coming Home Poems

(East Haven: LongRiver Books, 1986)

Like Beads

for Floyce

There is something stuck in my laughter,
language worn thin by summers, churning.

The steadiness of your eyes
calms me.

I weep for a lost hand, the knuckles
taut against old bone.
I weep for hearts and livers,
piles of gold teeth, mountains of hair.

A woman stares at the eye
gouged from her brother's human face,
my fist-sized muscle
thunders against your voice.

Time becomes old words, then shatters
as we walk through
planting our feet on sand that moves.

Days to be counted off the round stone
like beads in the hand
of a woman who photographs her own death.

A scenario replayed against Managua's open fields,
against her mouth, a wound.

I speak to you now from the Margaret in my throat.

Managua, December, 1983

Star 80

The man on the screen was going to be someone
using the woman on the screen.
The man on the screen photographed a delectable object
endlessly.
(With me it was always partial. Partial.)
The mother knew
but her eyes vanished.
The man on the screen invented and blundered.
Then need cruised his body
and he bought a pardon.
(In my life it always seemed more like reality. So subtle.)
The woman on the screen saw herself changing
according to the rules
and traveled an old road. The sun came out. Briefly.
Then the man without a history bought a gun.
Everything had already happened
as many times as there are pores in my body.
And it happened again.
Pity occupied another house.
The sound was explosive
and final.

I sat very still.
They pushed my head against the seat
hard.
My hands grew cold. Then hot.
In each of my body's pores
memory lit a single candle.
Wax smothered the pore.
Still, I burned.
Pain moved like music
as each receding image filled

with my exact experience.
Everything hurt more.
I felt old
from so much pain.

In my seat I did not want to rise.
I wanted to wait
for the answer.

Albuquerque, February 1984

Myself, Regrouping

These are my hands. Here they are.
Good hands, large
and strong.
Hands that have written poems
brought children to the world,
made love
and war.
In dreams they often race
or grow beyond their boundaries.
In dreams they have been black
as well as cold.

These are my feet. Also large.
Spread flattened for years
in crude sandals.
Lately, through re-entry,
shod with intimidating boots.
I like the intimidation.
It balances the smiles.

This is my smile. Sometimes
it fears exposure,
more often it breaks and tumbles
beyond the confines of my mouth.
In your mouth's upturned corners
it has found a friend.
Tongue to tongue. Tooth to tooth.
When your smile comes small
and stops
mine longs to move up close,
hold and complete your process.

I have strong legs, thighs that seize
and clasp,
broad hips belly breasts
marked by babies and by years.
Elbows that never wait by windows anymore
but often stump a silent keyboard
caress their own body's fingers
holding myself.

My fingers. They are light-sensitive
and live in history's mouth.
My nose has been called patrician
by some,
elephant snout by a boy in seventh grade
whose taunt I'm only now forgetting.
My hair has been braided dark brown
teased in the hesitant years
dyed a while in the bridging years
reclaiming its silver fire.

I have been told my eyes can see
and yes, they can.
They see and see and sometimes do not close
even when I will them to.
A third eye opens and shuts around my neck,
my camera's lens
ready and waiting on my skin.

I have two voices, tongues
with which to ask and say.
Sometimes my Latina high
lilts against the guttural deepness
of my Jewish shadowland.
A questioning Spanish "no?"
moves restless

through reclaimed English:
Seville, Mexico, Havana,
Lima, Hanoi, Managua,
Scarsdale, Lower East Side, Albuquerque,
everywhere.

My ears are less than perfect
inherited with love from my father
(as are my gums).
My memory is shredded.
Memory...is the hardest part.
So easy to lose. So distant or so close.
Lately I spend half my life
trying to remember.

Four children
extensions of myself
though not possessed
nor held by me.
Their own eyes and hands,
their own feet
travel them out
and they return
completing my voice, a circle
turning.

This is the skin I shed
and the new one
pulling against my bones.
This is my pain.
I claim it too
and offer it along with deepest love
and gift and remedy.

Albuquerque, March 1985

The Gloves

for Rhoda

Yes we did march around somewhere and yes it was cold,
we shared our gloves because we had a pair between us
and a New York city cop also shared his big gloves
with me–strange,
he was there to keep our order
and he could do that
and I could take that
back then.
We were marching for the Santa María, Rhoda,
a Portuguese ship whose crew had mutinied.
They demanded asylum in Goulart's Brazil
and we marched in support of that demand,
in winter, in New York City,
back and forth before the Portuguese Consulate,
Rockefeller Center, 1961.
I gauge the date by my first child
–Gregory was born late in 1960– as I gauge
so many dates by the first, the second, the third, the fourth,
and I feel his body now, again, close to my breast,
held against cold to our strong steps of dignity.
That was my first public protest, Rhoda,
strange you should retrieve it now
in a letter out of this love of ours
alive these many years.
How many protests since that one, how many
marches and rallies
for greater causes, larger wars, deeper wounds
cleansed or untouched by our rage.
Today a cop would never unbuckle his gloves
and press them around my blue-red hands.

Today a baby held to breast
would be a child of my child, a generation removed.
The world is older and I in it
am older,
burning, slower, with the same passions.
The passions are older and so I am also younger
for knowing them more deeply and moving in them
pregnant with fear and fighting.
The gloves are still there, in the cold,
passing from hand to hand.

Immigration Law

When I ask the experts
"how much time do I have"
I don't want an answer in years
or arguments.

I must know if there are hours enough
to mend this relationship,
see a book all the way to its birthing,
stand beside my father
on his journey.

I want to know how many seasons of chamisa
will be yellow and grey-green
and yellow
        /light/
             again,
how many red cactus flowers
will bloom beside my door.

I do not want to follow language
like a dog with its tail between its legs.

I need time equated with music,
hours rising in bread,
years deep from connections.

The present always holds a tremor of the past.

Give me a handful of future
to rub against my lips.

Albuquerque, October, 1985

Talk to Me

Talk to me. Three
words
moving with heavy feet
across the open spaces.

A signal,
or the beginning of a poem.

Talk to me. Not meaning
"how are things going?" Not meaning
"they can't do this to you"
(they can, they are)
not even
"what can I do to help?"

Do it, that's all.
Please.
No more questions, no more
knowledgeable statements.

Three words. Begin a poem. Take your life
and use it.

Albuquerque, Winter, 1986

FROM

Memory Says Yes

(Willimantic, CT: Curbstone Press, 1988)

Under the Stairs

My childhood place beneath the family's stairs
was home to Mr. Beeuff, Miss Level, Camp, Girlie—
faithful friends who came
when there was no one else.
Instantly available, invisible eyes
unprimed to take them in
or on.

We talked endlessly then
through years when Radio let imagination live
and presidents still died natural deaths.

Mr. Beeuff and Miss Level were adults. Ageless
in maturity and sedentary power.
His lined face and lunch pail.
She a nurse in crisp white service.
Years, then, of righteous wars, defense plants
and defense of honor.
Her hands were always clean.

Camp wore a leather jacket, rode a motorcycle,
was my male hero. Power and comfort
in the same breath.
Girlie was just that, his girl,
pliant pretty in whatever image of pretty
lit my eight-year-old eyes.
"No ideas but in things," Williams would say,
but what of ourselves as things? What about service?

When I asked about Pearl Harbor
my friends told me war was o.k.

Not to worry, as the saying goes. Today,
my own wars vying for room inside my chest,
I trace murky reason to those ready answers.

My body is just now my own. My pain
sits toward the back of the theatre. Chewing its nails.

Roque rides a bus, heavy volume of Che
on his jostling lap. He laughs.
How often now has the thousand dollars for Alvaro
changed hands?
Alvaro, José Benito,
interchangeable names in the single focus of death.

Liz says it's true, years ago she was shy
and had to work hard to bridge the deficit.
Debts never cancelled somehow, debtors
still looking for a place to stand up,
a place to say: I am.
When the body goes, can we say our work is done?

Mr. Beeuf might be a P-Niner now, his lunch pail
tired of the old liverwurst sandwiches,
pickles and chips.
Miss Level will not deal well
with memories of raging skin, pieces of bodies
cracking her memory
after Korea. After Vietnam, El Salvador.
Camp chooses himself. Girlie remains size eight.

Carlos' blue eyes pierce my poem,
Violeta's wound opens again and again
in my own right temple.
Light fades from Havana's seawall, brightens
over my mountain, whimpering in my hands.

We are always going home, going home
wherever memory stands up, says
it's time now. Right now it's time.

On days like these I take the silence
and the sweetness of these men and women
crowding my memory
waking through the cold of that
which is empty, unfinished.
I grab their breath, their teeth,
and tell them what I've learned:

It's not true
a child has no memory before the age of two.
You cannot solve the problems of the planet
in the space for lovers
but lovers can live in the world
if they work at it.
Dignity has bone, muscle.
There is no such thing as absolute truth.

We talk awhile, under the stairs.
I talk and listen as I did then.
They come and go as then.

All Last Week

for my daughter, Ana

All last week you preened before the mirror
viewing emerging breasts, then covering them
with gauze-thin blouse
and grinning: getting bigger, huh?

The week before you wore army fatigues
leveling breasts and teenage freckles,
tawny fuzz along your legs. A woman. Beginning.

Today you don fatigues again.
Today you pack knapsack and canteen,
lace boots over heavy socks
and answer the call Reagan and Haig
have slung at your 12 years.

Yours and so many others
–kids 14, 15, 18, so many others who will go
and some of them stay, their mothers
shouting before the Honduran Embassy:
"Give us our sons' bodies back,
give us back their bodies!" At least that.

All last week you preened before the mirror,
moving loose to new rhythms
long weekend nights. Junior High math. Sunday beach.
Today you go off
to the staccato of continuous news dispatches.
And I, in my trench, carry your young breasts
in my proud and lonely eyes.

Managua, March 1982

Remaining Option

I

My temperature goes up
and "who can measure the heat and violence
of the poet's heart
when caught in a woman's body?"
Virginia Woolf asked that
and went to sleep in her cold river.
Sexton and Plath, Santamaría and Parra
left abruptly
breaking the barrier of heat as someone or something
called in a voice louder than the heart.

Sexton started me down this road today
telling me Ann Frank was the Joan of Arc of Amsterdam.
A different kind of death.
And Ronnie Gilbert, singing
"The water is wide...I cannot cross."
It is wide but I can cross,
am crossing now, falling against the waves,
hoisting myself aboard the craft once more, going on.
Wet but warmed to this place
where a lagging heat divides and pulls me together again.

II

On the silver road last night
I stopped my car.
Stopped and pulled over, pulling my body
into its own curve,
hugging arms, thighs, ribs.

A shoulder was caught in the silent blade
of my windshield wiper.

The night was calm.
Fingers splayed against the glass
and the ancient bridle of an 18th century mount
was crushed beneath the front wheel
when I emerged desperate for air.

These are the fingers of war, the shoulders of war,
the bridle of unjust death,
fragments of fear.
These pieces of my mind
that will not stay behind
nor wilt.

III

Temperature and music
make room for the heart.
Memory presses against canyon walls
chipping the dark side of flight.

I am crossing now. Oh yes,
I am crossing.

Albuquerque, April 1985

The Green Clothes Hamper

Rain almost hides my mountains today.
Low clouds snag the rocky skirts, colors
of rain and clouds clean everything.

I speak of the rain, the clouds, the living
colors of this land
because it seems impossible to cut this silence with the words

my grandfather was a sick and evil man
posing as healer.
Now I retrieve his hands and eyes, his penis
filling my tiny infant mouth

as he forced himself into a body, mine,
that still finds reason easier than feeling.
Here is the green lucite top
of a clothes hamper where rape impaled diapers.

Here is memory catching up with itself,
overtaking asthma, compulsive food, fear
of that which is not itself.
This lost green hamper. My body coming home.

Albuquerque, Spring 1986

Variations on the Door

With Adrienne Rich

There is nothing I would not give
for years or even minutes,
time moving differently in this place we occupy,
memory hoisting itself upright in us.

There is nothing I would not give
you or another,
repetition comforts me today,
a long delicate line of pink light parts the sky
and a coyote crossing the road makes you smile.

Knowing you here —a here
distant as voices or a room apart
(working as I work)
our air becoming a single air—
knowing you here holds my body in space,
fixes my mind.

This knowledge neither linear nor perfect
is again and again the door
opening because we have chosen
to walk through, chosen to risk,
remember our names.

Memory walks tall in this dream, memory
and hope.
Nothing can call me home, love,
but to your eyes and hands.

Albuquerque, Winter 1987

Control

If she watched the good cowboys
and the bad injuns
on a screen that entered her mind and stayed
you may believe that mirrors cut her Indian face.
Light brown, she passed.
Latina, only her English syllables survived.
A woman, she was as much a man as any man
then as much of a woman was left to her to know.
A story emerged in shoulders like her own.
Woman-loving, she didn't exist
until she invented herself.

If she slouches now
you may be sure she was told to sit up
more than once. And that it was important.
If she always agrees,
we are correct in imagining
things were not what they seemed.
Not what they seemed to be
at all.

At a table of broken manners
she sits before a plate piled high
of rancid food.
There is gravy in her hair.
She practiced hard at being agreeable
so only smiles weakly
when armies of bloated bellies
are hired to do the dishes.
She herself will pay them. In flowers.

When she goes home at last
she will have to take her history
from her pocket,
spit and polish the map,
speak in tongues
and gently insist upon that skin
until anger is born in her eyes,
healing her wounds, turning her flesh
to earth.

Albuquerque, September–October 1985

FROM

Dancing with the Doe: New and Selected Poems, 1986-1991

(Albuquerque: West End Press, 1992)

I Want the Words Back

for Ruth Salvaggio

The words we wrote for generations in the caves
I want those words of ours.
Christendom's women ministering to the hungry
until Constantine cut off your priestly hands.
Sappho's lesbian call is what I want,
imprint of desire on those island rocks.
Pocahontas, la Malinche:
your stories wronged upside our throats
when told by men who could not sift
the wisdom from betrayal. I want you all.

Old nouns, safe between my fingers,
uncurl their sleeping bodies,
tell us who we were
before the patriarchs erased us in their fear.
I want to talk about our language,
how they changed it on us running.
Our gardens went untended then.
In pain, still taken by surprise,
we learned about not talking back, never
to look for home.

Micaela of the Andes, half a millennium
your military brilliance sings
through execution in a public square.
With four white horses
the conquerors pulled limb from limb that day.
Ripping tongue from mouth they believed
your punishment would stay a woman's language.

High villages still mourn
the loss of your resistance.

Namibian sisters, I want the lullaby
that strokes your babies' slumber—
memory of music and of milk.
Women stolen into slavery:
give me your coded song
through those forests where Diaspora's family
gathers to board the moving train.
Slaves and refugees continue
to cross those nights, still wait in silent barns
for your blue words.

Woman of Huehuetenango, slip me the words
you give your unborn child,
Quiché path of roots and leaves,
smallest and most valuable of animals,
ground corn, pungent before the day's first light.
Survival is blood of your tongue as of your cord.
As you carry your child through mountains
scarred by this new holocaust
you ask forgiveness of the earth.
Together let us whisper the dangers and the strength
that life demands.

Arkansas woman who would not tell your husband
how you cast your vote,
I need your silence
in a time when "no" meant "no."
He, splaying his drunken plea.
You, unbent against his hands
as women have always nurtured wordlessness.
Years pass, and bottles. Again
he will batter and leave you at your lonely washtub

with the children you must dream away.
Still you do not tell him how you placed your mark.

Today a new language stands up in us, its syllables
unwind these bandages of fear
that catch us frozen high above our bodies
or invisible behind the bedroom door.
Those who are always protected
cut and twist and accommodate a shame
not ours but theirs.
What I did not tell because he told me not to.
What would happen if I did.
And who would have believed me
anyway.

In dream ancestral words anoint our woman's life.
Blood surfaces through corrosive history.
We hold the thundering tongues, those names
that are walking sticks or amulets.
Reborn from silenced myth
we ready our mouths.
We speak.

The Colors of my Language

Language stood defiant in that house
where colors dripped
from syllables I learned to speak
between soft fingers of flesh
and corners where the scale of broken notes
rocked limbs of milk,
full prism of my earliest picture book.

Once a heart peeled back its stripes of meaning
and wild pink lit my secret place
beneath the stairs
where four imagined friends
brought solace in:
dulled black folds of the leather jacket
Mr. Beuff wore, Miss Level's nursely white,
Camp's tan and the springy tarnished gold
of Girlie's honey curls.

Much later, real children came
to walk beside me: Gregory's long purple
streaked with shots of turquoise blue.
Sarah the multicolor of Girlie's hair.
Ximena iridescent as she turns away
and Ana's name
brightening red sequins in a sea of brown.

In that house where I was daughter
brick-browns danced rhythms of adult people,
half-words beneath the shrouded balcony
where I crouched with little sisters
complicitous behind coarse drapes,
listening to Mama's puzzle of forbidden talk:

the creamy strand of sex words,
orange commas and exclamation marks
crowding the plaid and navy of those years.
Today my lover's tan and teal are here
to cradle my shoulders' homing.

My agate brother would come later,
leaping to where I stand.
Back then it was all green,
the flash of Girl Scouts, pearly knife
I lusted for and finally took
from our village five & dime.
Mother dragged me head bowed down gray Main Street
to confess in ocher tones the lie, the grief,
the history unraveled at my feet.

Deep red is my Margaret name, and the Meg
–for Little Women– a paler red,
old T-shirt worn for comfort
on the fighting days. Layers of black
hold me where I become myself,
keep me from fear of Grandpa's tongue
as I finger the satin binding of a winter blanket,
soft orange brought out each year
to calm my watchful eyes.

Today all love remains the color of ripe peaches
mottled in the high months.
Their juices wet my mouth
with the pale dust of a cracked moon.
Our wars defy this rainbow of harsh syllables,
their cold fires blind the child's eye
still peering from my face.

In this house where I am mother
again —grandmother, lover—
what I know is: colors change.
Nothing is primary or unmoved.
Barbara, pale green one day
then flat yellow or sparkling blue,
holds me like the shadows on our mountain:
great wings, birds
changing color as they fly and stay.

Jesse Helms and my Grandfather

The night we couldn't vote Jesse Helms from office
I dreamt of my grandfather.
His pale eyes pierced the safety of my bed
and I woke to a closed morning,
joy a dying flame
snuffed between the fingers of my left hand.
Out of sleep I moved to your warm back, love,
seeking comfort like old radio themes, familiar speech.

Grandpa in the bedroom. Jesse in my fear. In the dream
their faces flash on and off and on
like some neon sign: alternating images
from a single source. Grandpa's, magnified,
still stalks a child who cannot speak.
Grandma, standing in the shadow of an open door
observes his power, counts my loss
upon her rosary of sad complaints.

She was a whiner, that woman, but not even whining
did she let his secrets out. When I was two.
When I was six. Standup memory
tearing at my lips, my temperature up
when I was fourteen, thirty-seven, forty-nine.
Time, moving in all directions.

It comes into focus like rape on a TV screen
when soldiers go where they should not be,
kill and die for men in white houses.
As war rises in our throats
invasion's last mortar fire
falls broken from between our legs.

Jesse says, *They ain't seen nothin' yet!*
Grandpa fidgets in my sleep.
Your back a map of open country,
safety beneath my palms.
Survival, moving in all directions
and rising between my ribs, is mine.

Yes, Something *Did* Happen in my Childhood

I am a cook for others, a shameless feeder
of lovers, children, friends.
I plead guilty to this destiny or daily task,
this knowledge running from the succulent pores
of a pork roast
lodged in the aftertaste of curry stew,
rising in weekly dough of warm bread.
I give food as sustenance, stake well my territory,
unnerving tempers I spoon advice
to challenge hearts and minds.
On cold mornings I sit with recipe books
(*The Joy of Cooking* lived and died
five lifetimes in my hands).
There are full-color gourmet photographs,
I preview heady scrapings from a bowl or pan,
my energies rush to the fore
when no one waits or wishes to be served.
I am the woman over-filler of mouths,
that plate-heaper learning late
to let my eaters serve themselves,
come back for seconds on their own terms.
My food is not for thought
but for the belly, belt unbuckled,
every diet plan on hold.
I am the writer, teacher, political activist
who dreams of high praise for my apple pie,
a note in the *Times Book Review*
for my oven-baked chicken enchiladas.
Yes, something *did* happen in my childhood.
No, I can't remember what it was.

Dancing with the Doe

Each time I relearn dignity one tawny deer
stops tall, then leaps and poses motionless
at the edge of this meadow
darkened by its loss of day.
Bruising the hearty muscle in my breast
it fades to the forest I cannot enter from my fear.

Some days she is fawn, large head
on her perfect body
and soft white spots.
Then she is doe
running with other does,
or the image of one thunderous buck
charging the waters that reshape this land,
its furious grace.

Someone tells a slender friend
she has lost weight
and the friend says *thank you.*
Buck or fawn rears silent in my throat.
It is I who am saying thank you, thank you,
words drumming beneath my skin.
And we continue to turn the glossy pages,
strut to the piper's tune, a message
whose tiny belts squeeze hourglass waists
on cans of liquid promise.

Today I dance with the doe.
But I am also buck and fawn
slow motion spiraling and powerful arms
dancing myself in place.

In place in history.
In place in time.
Now the forest unfolds to my eyes
that leap through its secrets like stars.

The Path that Disappears

When we climb our mountain, she says,
with incense and flowers,
her eyes somewhere up there above our heads,
when we follow the path we knew
but do not show respect,
the path itself will disappear.

Everywhere in these highlands they say,
The Invasion.
Outsider, I remember the early eighties,
Lucas García, Ríos Montt, Church of the Word.
442 villages disappeared, a blasphemed map.
Erasing the infant at his mother's breast,
loss of chickens and new corn.

I remember Guatemala 1954, our CIA
when the word *Communist*
brought efficient response.
Their destiny manifest in ours.
Ten years before I remember
a dress rehearsal in shadow time.

But she remembers 1492.
The first invasion, heavy corroding
five centuries, breaking memory,
murdering language in the throat.
Rape of air, earth, child,
this place once safe for life.

Resistance cuts and runs
where names cannot bear the weight
of pale men on horses, terror

of the cross.
Here we are the image of that first invasion
echoing each new death.

Now our women's voices
punctuate this mouth gone dry
that tries to speak.
Together,
here,
we call our separate memories up
this side of rage.

We did not need your discovery, she says,
and holds out both her open hands.

Grief in, not In Front Of, the Mirror

I

Nothing in your language or the tiny lines around your eyes
prepares me for that other, colder hour
when, years beyond our mist-swept promontory,
news of your death frames memory.
A liberated land where both of us are guests.
I am grieving now, with a grief no island can sustain.

I have only to place my hands on a stripe of Cuban sand
to haul up this image of brilliant sun.
Burning, alive,
it holds a picture of poets
gathered in DuPont's abandoned mansion
sharing a mystery that crowns
between the thighs of two colliding worlds.

Paco, you told me about home, Argentina,
war draining the light from your squared fingers.
Roque was with us then, and Rodolfo,
inhabiting the shared certainty
of children wild with all our dreams.
That day the pain of a tropic dance slow-motioned us
around the words that did not fit our mouths.

Again, I retrieve the final image: the door
of your house swings open violently.
It is a particular house, a particular day
in history. Your last.
They, surrounding the single warrior.
You, emerging in a storyteller's burst of fire,
your weapon coughing and spitting as you go down.

II

This year I teach in DuPont country.
Everywhere I feel upon my skin
the tycoon's taste and table,
daughters who bring their name
to marriage vows,
a family that owns the state of Delaware.

South Africa? This university will not divest,
for DuPont in Johannesburg
is like Bush in Kuwait–
that logic of owners who swiftly nod their heads
in places they have made their own.

The old man's inbred son
bought rooms like lives from unsuspecting houses.
I mean whole rooms: ceilings, walls,
the sterling fixtures of a lesser people's world.
This museum, once his home,
has more than two hundred such displays.

On the streets people say they are lucky
to work for the biggest boss,
lucky to live by his cold patronage
and reputable greed.
All manner of conformities profit in these times.

III

Paco, in Buenos Aires your war is history now
but a plaza embraces brave grandmothers
still patrolling the genes of babies
wrenched from the wombs

of those who were tortured twice:
dead first in the bodies of their children
and again by their own lonely names.

This hour the two of us share broken metaphors
in that scorching island sun.
I, a poet left among the living,
grieve for the children in our poems,
they who believed us when we said
we would divide the sun in equal portions.
Now *their* children stumble through our dreams.

In Cuba a single white egret
stands motionless upon the grass.
Your dead eyes
and mine that race awkwardly to catch up
meet in the stillness of that bird.

Somewhere
a young poet struggles again with the first line
of a poem of the world, waiting.

A Poem in Praise of Free Enterprise

1

Is it true that you modeled nude for artists,
waitressed in a gay bar in the decade of the fifties?
Why did the magazine you edited print an ad
for a bookstore that sold Marxist books?
How did you feel, publishing poems
in a magazine that also published Communists?
Tell me, Ms. Randall, did you ever write
a poem in praise of free enterprise?

2

Free
enterprise, the
enterprise of freedom
or
enter here: a prize to empower our own
our own enterprise
of freedom
which is anything but
that bawdy concept
pressing dry
the juices of our lives.

3

Now that the words spoken in that courtroom
are faint static on their circular journey,
now that this line of questioning gone stale

evokes no more than sorry images,
self-righteous or self-conscious jabs,
courtroom suit pressed into service,
virulent pokes at tired dignity,
now that you've lost and we've won
I thought I'd try my hand at that poem
in praise of free enterprise.

4

You know, I've never been good
at what they call occasional verse
but then this is never occasion
so much as reflection upon the state of poetry
in times when freedom to evoke or sing
must go to court.

5

Is it not true…?
Why…?
How did it feel…?
Did you
*ever write a poem
in praise of free enterprise?*

No.
But will this do:

Please join me in a cry or song
to the enterprise of freedom,
to the process of reorganizing need,
looking need squarely in the eye

and finding
things are not what they should be, could be,
please join me in this rage,
decision to fight and be.
Our enterprise, breathing to be free.
Join me, please,
in this daily practice,
the quiet rhythm of our hands.
The quiet rhythm of all our hands.

Driving with Daddy

Too small in the seat and tired
shrunken into yourself
eyes strained to the road
you will not turn your head
as you say
You'll have to tell me where to turn.

I will, daddy. I'll tell you
where to turn,
never prepared for this
speaking loud to your deafness
your concentrated profile
behind the wheel.

Mother in the back seat
tells you when to pass.
She tells you wrong, pleads
I never do anything right.

Each shifting of gears
is complex slow motion:
push the stick in so…
clutch to the floor…
across and down, or up.

Instruction from forty years before
when you taught your oldest daughter
how to drive
and I sat at the edge of the seat
feet barely touching the pedals.

I was your daughter, you my father
and you so big then.
Did I sleep when we passed
moving apart?
Daddy, I am riding now
on the power of my life
as you recede.

Quick in my throat
your gentle hand on mine
through early failures
memory floating, turning,
turned to annoyance:
numbers just won't balance anymore,
fact or figure straying from you head.

Your burst of anger,
what people do to one another
on this earth...
cracking to let a phrase or gesture through.
Upright. Forthcoming still.

Bent beneath the pain
of the son who left his wife
my own uncertain status
long distance once a week
with your other daughter
in another state.

Grandchildren coming too fast
upon your cheek,
it all adds up
to something long expected, balanced,
about to fall?

I wanted to keep it together you said
in spite of everything,
keep it together.
And you did.

Thick as Honest Memory

My father's thick hand holds mine
and I his.
We are wind chill 18 degrees one hungry lung
who must believe our lives against this war.

Mother stands apart inside the glass doors
hiding from cold,
her thin body stiff as all the barricaded words.
Trouble is, she says, *we can't make a difference.*
Nothing will change.

My father's hand in mine does trust
a sudden shift in weather
his fingers thick as honey, honest memory.

Years I have leaned into his holding
against all language of shame.
Today's paper says six hundred
but we know that many thousands gather here
protesting unjust war. Between our touching fingertips.

Joel Oppenheimer 1930-1988

The strong wife of my firstborn's father
calls to tell us it's time.
Tomorrow or the next day
a week at most.
He talks and is not in pain,
has prepared well to die.

And you? I ask.
There's no preparing...
I search for words.
Come on, you're the poet,
she challenges my craft, laughs.
Tears gripping this wire
between women who have never met.

The children's visit meant so much,
tell them they're stuck with me...
Her voice is warm
from New Hampshire's first signs of winter.
Here, on this autumn desert
feathery Apache plume and flowering sage
it is almost dusk.
Two a.m. in Paris
where my son picks up the phone.
I have moved through my tears,
relay the message.

Time zones and languages contract, expand,
replay the shared granddaughter
just now completing
the cycle of her first year.

We are poets who walked briefly
in each other's lives,
grow old in New Hampshire, New Mexico,
our children and their children
testing the words we leave behind.

May the words grow with them
and keep singing, Joel,
crossing time zones
powerful against corrupt statistics,
beaten babies, lies
that fake this rallying beat of truth.

No one is fooled.
Death only lives
when the language of life is gone.

The Morning I Dreamed my Children

for Audre Lorde

The morning I dreamed my children lingers, I dreamed
them dead.
It was with me morning to morning
and all the nights
compressed,
a place of rupture sealed shut.

This morning I came from sleep at five
knowing it was seven where you are
a good time
to start your name on energy waves
my lips to your hospital bed
a movement of gurneys, hanging bottles,
intrusions *their* way.

Making corrections I whispered
Audre...Audre...Audre...Audre...
into my sheets then out onto air
a sound that would move towards you,
take you, hold you

from sisters and brothers who know
"we need those who work"
as Sonia said, "those who work..."
and voices: "Teach it, sister!"
coming from other Black women mostly and

from others of us learning,
learning to learn.
This morning it was time

one more of our times of trial
and I sang *Audre*

louder 'til the wind caught vowels
and they stood, thick fabric of tone
swollen for life
like the morning I dreamed my children dead
then dreamed them back.

Now their names rise: Gregory…Sarah…Ximena…Ana…
Barbara…Audre…Audre…Francis and Winnie…
Guadalupe…Dora María…Rosa's ghost,
the ones who work
oh the ones who work in me.

The Suicide Wheel

1

It's happened again. A young woman says I can't
and overdoses on regret.
Pillage cries in her veins like the low squares
of an Anasazi ruin.
She would sweep them clean but she's tired,
the language of power backed up in her like silt.

Attempted suicide. From a heavy sea,
words that tear a hole in the temperature of bone,
in the hand-held mirror of our hunger
cracking the songs we knew by heart.
A great chorus of crickets renting this night in heat.

Gas, blades, pills were never enough
or didn't work.
Wrong shadows fall across her hands,
death's name is harbored in too small a voice.
Life, she of the strong teeth and obstinate muscle,
waits broken on the foreign side of shame.

Where are the letters that will become this word?
Silence and choice fight here with kitchen knives.

II

I will take you to pentimento suicides.
Chosen, they surface now through layered paint,
insistent images.
Vladimir Mayakovski,

                    Haydée Santamaría,
within a year of Haydée
Beatrice Allende also dead.

The first leans towards me in an old photograph,
his nation baffled, a salt taste.
In Haydée's eyes I see myself
carved from sacred soapstone, waiting.

A music maker joins these three
in a song he calls The Suicides
and asks
if we must tremble upon their common territory.

I tell him I don't know.
In my graying eyes the Russian poet
will forever hitch his trouser
tall in clouds.
Indelible I hear my Cuban heroine say:
When I had to send them out to kill
I always chose the ones I knew would hate the job.
And in the Comrade President's daughter's perfect shot
Chile is bared once more, a bloodied rendering.

III

Sea warms about us, holds
to its old story.
Sometimes no more than the present tense
is left of this Monday morning
incapable of lies.

It's all right, I say, there's time
to die or live.

Where choice stumbles, a broken amulet
may become raw memory,
blackbirds rankling and cawing at your throat.

There will always be kitchens, always knives,
but feathers and leaves rise like swirls of dust
when we take choice, love it, coax or drag it home.
Death chosen is not silence
and memory never death when you set it beating,
heartful of language, in your mouth.

This Energy Flashing and Singing

for Meridel Le Sueur,
at ninety

Do you remember when we crossed
in the rhythm of a freight train
moving west?
You were a woman of the range
strong-jawed, laughing.
I was a child
half hidden behind my mother's
dark green skirt.
Or maybe I stood in a lonely field
at the end of one of those sparse towns
I sometimes come upon today,
always wondering what it would be like
to have been born there,
to have grown in a place like that:
isolate, dusty, smelling only of wind.
You waved and your energy was breath to me.

What color is your rage?
Does the future feel safer
or less safe?
Is tomorrow still another day?
What about the houses,
rooms inhabited now by strangers?
What about this silence
filled to the brim with sound?
Do unacknowledged victories
still shimmer in the night?
persistent fireflies?
History is a thin dog

scavenging through yesterday's garbage.
Where do the piles of Jewish teeth and hair
meet Palestinian stones
flung by children's hands
across dulled paths of memory?

Where are the yellow stars and pink triangles,
the underwear of pestilence, slow cough of fear?
Where the whisper of famine on this land?
What about earth, water, air,
those who were here
when The Man came and came again?
When will big nations respects small nations
for the first time?
Battered woman, raped sister,
where are the disappeared, their shirts and names?
Will newscasters ever stop telling us
DeKlerk released Mandela,
admit he fought his 27 cruel years out of prison,
a people in search of life?

Meridel, here is pain in process
and process itself stands taller for me now.
Is this what happens
when the years peel back their branches,
human core burst tender in such heat?
A baby's flesh
but succulent and wise,
this last delicate garden.
Once you spoke to me of age
like rot, decay, a living phosphorescence.
Life giving birth to itself
by its own proximity with death.
Is this what you meant by process?
This energy flashing and singing its way

through spitfire winters
rising with the sun?

Meridel, when I tried to come home
and they closed the door
everyone lamented
but you said *Bravo*!
If they'd let you in
you never would have lived it down!
I closed my eyes and dreamed of warm rain
then woke with rebel patience in my mouth,
a medicine bag of courage at my waist.
Of course: I had wanted what isn't theirs to give.
You taught me once again
that victories are born of old boots
and savage shoulders,
the stuff of struggle.
When finally they turned broken in defeat,
when I did come home,
your fighting litany rang lyric in my ear.

Your stories, Meridel,
they sleep in my elbows and belly,
stretch and rise when the fires burn low
and dry wood is nowhere to be found.
So much of our energy
comes from *your* energy,
so much of our great communal voice
reverberates from the words
you planted, plant, will go planting
across our hungry lips.
I reach and catch their echo in my hands.
Its waves crest and stream between my fingers
collected in little glowing pools of memory
about my feet.

You have taught us memory
from grandmother to mother
every woman a daughter
catching and weaving
a granddaughter
braiding her own hair.
And memory too from father to son
in brittle hope
as earth pursues its slow turn,
and men come wandering back
into the circle we prepare
and decorate in all our names.

You who have named our names:
today we come again, our infant sounds,
our syllables.
We leave you the grateful promise
of their journey in our eyes.
Ninety and grand,
you give us these colors,
replenish the taste of each,
so we may take them back once more,
move on.

Retablos for Frida

1

In Mexico I always visit your house.
I know you remember the blue house in Coyoacán
where your trickster spirit
still rises from every kitchen pot.

I always come back to the butterflies
stunned as your broken body
pinned in their glass case
on the underside of the last bed's canopy.

I stop before the papier-mâché Judas
that guards the entrance to your garden,
twenty-foot monster of betrayal,
his volcanic wall of ash.

2

Our cities are filled with homeless now—
men lead us into fabricated wars,
prepare to celebrate five centuries of occupation.
But of course you know all this.

I share today's calamity as I stare
at the portraits of Marx, Engels, Lenin, Stalin, Mao
fixed like soldiers at the foot of your bed.
And I smile, amused,
remembering you and Trotsky,
your private calendar in San Angel's secret rooms.

3

Dreaming, I wonder about the women
who lay down with you.
I search for the fire that must have seared your hands
when you and Tina hid behind each other's eyes.

Each morning's promise,
retablo for the day just ended
or the one exuberantly begun.

I too love people–women–
yet there are moments people, even women
wear me out.

4

Dying, you must have known the risk
of instant explanation: *frail…victim…
attempted suicide…*
They told such easy stories
of others in your time.

How quickly they bared
your shriveled leg,
your steel-pierced sex revealed to the world.

But then, how not to die
against so many doctors' orders,
pills, amputation, lies,
biographers whining down your door?

Frida, what recipe held you fast to life
when the energy to fix your ribboned hair was gone?

5

Ten years before you went
you dreamt a swirling sunflower
yellow aura of flames
fanned out from your sudden upright face.

That dream became prophecy.

As your body on its pallet slid forward
towards the crematorium's mouth
heat jackknifed muscles and you sat up
eyes open
riding hard into the furnace
that would change your molecules.

6

Frida, my flesh, too defies me.
Often it hauls forth
its own memories of great empty holes.

Then I remember Hermenegildo Bustos
painter of portraits
dead in Guanajuato just days before your birth.

7

Ten days before your death you marched
(in your wheelchair, a wrinkled scarf
hiding the hair you could no longer braid)
pollen of conquered pain already softening your eyes,
Guatemala raised in your tired fist.

8

There is always Diego, your *saporana*
green frog child
suckling dry the mother's breast.
He still traces history in our eyes
but knew you were the better painter
called you *fierce Mexican innocent.*

Frida, with you I keep
one last memory of your Diego
eyes bulging through tears
taking out his sketchbook
and drawing your shimmering skeleton
reaching for the flames.

When he died they did not mix his ashes
as he wished with yours.
Jealous wife and daughters,
anticommunism, fear of flames:
all had their hand in the poor rewrite.
He: carried off to the Circle of Illustrious Ones,
you: settled but restless in your dark clay pot.

9

Knife wounds, little fountains of blood,
twin spirits joined at your broken spine.
Gemini's double helix
will not reduce to one.

The two Frida's only feign their rest
in the closed circle of your unbreakable life.
Only your pain, your full heart and pain

live on in the blue house
and in my impatient rage.

I Am Loving You

for you, Barbara

I am loving you in the furrowed temperature
of our bodies broadening soft
moving into the trust we fashion
this day and the next.
Holding each other, our children
becoming grandchildren, our grandchildren
growing into this world we want to change,
its broken law of greed and pain.

I am talking about the curve of a breast
in this time when nothing is given
and almost everyone dies before her time.
A trill of sandhill cranes
hold captive breath and sky.
In some ancient cell I know our fingers
moved and touched, remembering.
Perhaps we were sisters, husband and wife,

perhaps we were mother and daughter
father and son, interchangeably.
In a future that requires
successful closure of the Salvadoran war,
all sides in the Middle East
to give something and get something,
I am loving you still
resting against your shoulder's heat.

I am loving you as the sun goes down in Matagalpa,
women like us stroking each other
in old high-ceilinged rooms, jacaranda patios

their walls pocked by the silent caliber
of old battles.
Sun rising over Johannesburg, over Belfast,
pale through a narrow ravine on Hopi land
where a child pushes her flock before her,
embracing herself against the wind.

Against the winds of change we shape the word
with our mouths that can say these things
because other women said them
and others dreamed them
looking then looking away
holding each other quickly, fear
standing at the door.

Pinatubo's fallout
turns the evening clouds a burning red
about this New Mexico desert
where I am loving you now
long and carefully slow
with words like *wait* and *here* and *yes*
as we tell each other
the world is still a dangerous place.

We will take it one death at a time
claiming only the memory
of our trembling and our rage.

FROM

Hunger's Table: Women, Food and Politics

(Watsonville, CA: Papier-Mâché Press, 1997)

Cold Ginger Chicken

Round tables gather a family in, reject
a father who commands the head, a mother
running to and from the kitchen
as courses replace one another
and conversations wane.

Mix fresh grated ginger, 4 cloves
grated garlic, rock salt
and olive oil. When sauce has blended,
cover and refrigerate at least 2 hours.
Square or rectangular tables

arrange and order a family, there is always
one who must keep her back to the wall,
another who cannot take direct sunlight
or naturally occupies the end
from which directives flow.

Boil chicken breasts about 10 minutes or
until just barely cooked. Remove from heat
and plunge into ice water. Skin. Cover
with plastic wrap and chill. When cold,
cut into 2-inch pieces. Arrange on a bed

of watercress, leaving a space in the center
for your bowl of sauce. One side, each end,
center or gentle diameter. Position
is everything when winter comes
and snow begins to fall.

Ingredients

1/2 cup fresh grated ginger
4 cloves grated garlic
1 teaspoon rock salt
1 cup olive oil

Bouillabaisse

You may use roughy or filet of sole,
delicate white fish flaking tender
to the nudge of a fork or old hunger.
Set aside the loaves and fishes
of our several memories.
Open your mouth. Wide. The world
crawls beneath your tongue.
Speak of famine and human need.
Nothing will disappear
before your breath quickens
and wise women sit at your table.

Cut the raw filets into bite-size pieces
and place them in a dish
already graced with large bay scallops.
Close your eyes. Remember your childhood dreams
of justice and deserved reward.
A steady stream of cool water
soothes your fingers
as they rinse and peel the shells
from large green shrimp. Twenty or 30.
They too go into the dish,
a mound of clean cold products of the sea.

Stop everything. Stand very still.
Think of the perfect dinner guest.
Her clear eyes look back at yours,
acknowledging the feast to come.
You might want snapper or salmon
though the latter will make a heavier soup.
Add mussels in their obsidian shells.
Bits of crab are delicacies.

Rings of cleaned squid
unusual and satisfying.

The dish of fresh seafood and fish
goes into the white refrigerator,
waits while we keep looking away
from those pictures of the world's starving,
deadened limbs reaching out,
eyes larger than the faces in which they shine.
Refuse to hold the images
without their counterpart of culture—
people making and doing.

Who are they? And still they starve. And still,
this is how we prepare to eat—
accepting them clean of their history,
their halved voice.
In a deep soup pot heat 1/4 cup olive oil.
Add 1/2 cup finely chopped onion,
stirring until translucent but not browned.
Throw in 8 or 10 plump garlic cloves,
peeled and minced.

A teaspoon dark red saffron strands,
a teaspoon grated orange rind,
another of freshly ground white pepper,
and a tablespoon finely chopped fresh fennel.
A pinch of celery or fennel seed, a bit of basil.
Stir in 4 to 5 peeled tomatoes
and 2 or 3 tablespoons tomato paste.
A cup chopped fresh parsley is optional,
your garden earth.
And finally salt, that lively grain of the sea—
a couple of teaspoons, or to taste.
Stir often.

We are almost ready now.
Our hands almost touch,
reaching across an ocean of greed and ache,
claiming the images in these eyes,
ours and theirs. We are almost finished
pretending they are not part of us,
or we of them.

To the vegetables add 6 cups fish stock
or water, and allow to simmer an hour or so
until the soup is eaten.
Five minutes before you bring it to the table
add the fish and seafood,
stirring over a raised flame
until they are just done.
Pink shrimp, scallops an opaque white
–tender but never overcooked.

Ladle the bouillabaisse over thin slices
of toasted garlic bread, one to a bowl,
or accompany with steamed white rice.
The bowls may be cobalt blue
or cadmium red.
Green salad or creamed spinach,
white wine, fresh pears with hot brie
make a good dessert.
Nothing will chide us
but those great eyes staring
from the bottom of pot or plate,
a numbed request where nothing but silence
stood.

Play discreet music now,
or garnish with lively conversation,
unrehearsed.

Potato Latkes

There is nothing quite like this taste,
my hand and mouth,
a winter evening in Manhattan.
You have given yourself a treat
because the uptown editor said no

to your first shy novel, because
he looked you over
benevolent behind his drink
and said go back to Albuquerque
get married and oh yes

have some kids. No one lives
where he wants you to go.
Steam rises from subway grates
and frost splits the atom
of this hunger strafed by memory.

Only a square of waxed paper
separates your fingers
from the sizzling batter,
just short of crisp but never soggy–
grated potatoes wrung dry
inside the clean white cloth,
three of them tossed with
flour, cream, some
grated onion, a beaten egg
and salt to taste.

Today I coat the skillet with
butter or bacon grease,
spoon the mixture to pancake size

and turn until golden
on each side.

Now I serve them with homemade
applesauce or sour cream.
Back then I paid for food
on the run, walked fast, dreamed
of ancestors who never used

the fat of swine. Those years
I devoured calendar and sustenance,
acknowledged a link
between the woman I imagined myself to be
and 14th Street's neon rush,

voices that begged: Sit down,
take a load off, stay a while.
I couldn't hear the meaning
of those words, didn't know
about Hannah, sister of Aaron

whose eyes took the camera defiant
and looked so much like mine.
Now I sit and eat, ponder
the apple-green sauce
or glistening sour of thick cream

against the crisscross gold.
I understand the words
and how they made me who I am.
We eat together slowly now.
Together and slowly.

Ingredients

3 peeled and grated potatoes wrung dry in a clean cloth
1 tablespoon flour
1 tablespoon cream
1/2 grated onion
1 beaten egg
salt to taste

Battered Woman Surprise

A recipe for baba ghannouj, a Near Eastern blend of
baked eggplant, tahini, parsley, garlic, and lemon, often
served with wedges of pita bread.

The great round purplish black eggplant
is quietly crazed in loneliness.
Not merely alone or needing space
but lonely in its full circumference.
Floating, burgundy, swollen in fear.

Prick her all over with the tines of a fork
then lay her directly on the rack
of an oven set to 400. In 45 minutes
she will shrink into herself, her polished skin
a defeated mass of wrinkles.

When cool enough to handle, scrape her flesh
to a bowl with 1/4 cup sesame tahini,
lots of pressed garlic, finely chopped
parsley, salt, pepper, and the juice
from at least two lemons.

Now her blue-black sheen is gone, her fullness
barely remembered. But this delicacy
—chilled aphrodisiac—
may be scooped into a little center bowl
surrounded by Wheat Thins or melba toast.

Before serving, drizzle a bit of olive oil
across the top. Guests will enjoy
the exotic taste you share with them.
And the appetizer —improved for its own good—
will not complain.

Canyon Food

for Dennise Gackstetter

"The first day I make too much food,"
you tell me.
"That lets people know they can come back for more.
Then they eat what they want, aren't anxious
about getting enough.
I have less waste and a measure of appetites."

Dennise, I have asked for your secrets,
how you learned to cook for twenty-four campers
forging 286 miles of furious river
through 1.7 billion years of wind and rock,
three thousand of human culture
and our own sixteen days.

You explain how everything has to be packed in,
all waste taken out.
I have seen each pristine campground welcome us,
done my part to leave them unspoiled
for travelers to come.

River water filtered through porcelain
when we drink,
pumped into pans or shot through with Clorox
when used to clean the dishes and mugs.
Long metal tables
that circumscribe your kitchen,
doubling as hatch covers,
waiting as backboards in case of emergency.

I have noticed your daily squares of paper,
lists for each boatman,
to forage for boxes of lettuce,
bags of chicken breasts, apples in buckets,
Oreo cookies and cheese,
coffee, vegetables, chocolate, clams.

Mike growing sprouts in the bottom of his dory.
Mary hauling silver tanks of butane.
The exuberance
of Shawn's fried fish tacos.
Jano putting her lips to a blue plastic toy,
sacred "trombat" calling us to dinner.

"It's all in the timing," you say,
"all about knowing how long
to simmer the rice,
when to light a fire beneath the vegetables
or set the salmon steaks to broil."
Hot coals cover your Dutch oven
raised on flattened beer cans, promise
of dessert again tonight.

"It's all in the timing."
You grin.
And I know you mean
the mammoth scale
slowing us down
allowing us to drift
from that constraint we call civilization,

trusting ourselves to fall backward
in our deepest appetites.

Antonio's Rice

It was plain white rice, scant ration of salt
to move us on. Cuba, the revolution's glory years
and still we had five pounds a month, a lot
you'll say, but think of it there on the plate
with nothing adorning its size.

He served it up in little mounds, formed by
filling one light green plastic coffee cup
then inverting its equity before each patient fork.
An egg or some *butifara* (hot dog-like sausage,
occasional treat) if things were good,

a ladle full of split pea soup if they were not.
How we joked about those split peas,
chícharos in every possible disguise.
Boil and throw the water out, boil again
and throw out the water, and again and again

until the punch line telling you to throw out
the peas. And also the pot.
Carmen whispered that version one early dawn
as we patrolled the block, arms swinging in unison,
collars raised against cold sea air.

Women keeping our neighborhood safe against crime,
invasion, or loneliness,
whatever threatened that nation
of spent cooks. Tomato sauce without tomatoes.
Marmalade made from boiling the mango skins.

Those hours the recipes came –an endless volley
against the dark sea wall, back and forth
between neighbors struggling to stay awake.
Antonio's rice was the stalwart,
the sure thing,

guaranteed to bring that beautiful fairness
into our home.

Mud of Heaven

for Stan Persky

My friend Stan has just published a book
about the fall of European Communism,
ordinary household objects failing
to keep the promises we demand of them.

He knows that eros is the beginning
of knowledge.
His young lovers are hustlers
not prostitutes, entrepreneurs not victims.
As he is not their victimizer.

Stan's male homo culture is neither backdrop
nor center stage for his explanation
of what gave way, finally, what fumbles now,
rebirthing itself at Tirana's Datji
or along the dissolving streets of Budapest.

"I have sort of stopped eating meat and pastries
though I don't yet notice any dramatic
shape difference," he writes me,
then asks if I have a poem
or recipe for chocolate mousse,
the Mud of Heaven as he calls it.

To Berlin's Fuggerstrasse I send instructions:
Sliver 6 squares semisweet chocolate,
a toss of salt and 2 tablespoons water
in a double boiler.
Stir until the chocolate is
meltdown smooth, a liquid lust.

Then beat 4 egg yolks to a light lemon color,
slowly combining with the chocolate.
Stir in 2 teaspoons vanilla extract
and beat the egg whites
with full knowledge of the task,
so they stand in soft peaks, yearning for sky.

Fold into the chocolate. Whip
and add your heaviest cream.
Spoon this mud of heaven into glasses
chilled until ready to serve.
More cream may be laced with sugar
and piled on top.

Six to eight hungry lovers satiate themselves
in this stirring and melting,
beating and whipping and yearning
and folding and spooning and cooling.
The fall of communism layers upon the tongue
in all its parts.

The memory of a young boy's back,
a statement of purpose
folded against the storm.

Hunger's Table

pain is not a flower, pain is root
–Paul Monette

Now they sleep with the plague
beneath their pillows:
dancers and teachers, doctors and florists,
truckers and lawyers and priests.
Now they duel with her night sweats,
remembering that they will soon forget,
and die with our love in tow.

        The woman I was
        keeps setting this table,
        announces she is putting
        forks to the left,
        knives and spoons to the right,
        petals of night bloom
        curling.

Your skin tells time, a map
inviting me to contemplate
the loss of gardens.
There is no choice when choice
commands you turn your back on passion.
Lover and teacher, writer and friend,
come sit at my table
while you are still able to dine
and a canyon wren floats transparent song.

        Water glasses are Mexican green,
        wine goblets rimmed in fire,
        dishes perfectly empty.

The woman I am
kicks off her shoes,
sits down to eat.
She thinks about
what taunts her on the plate,
devours its body,
repeats its name.

These are the years of love letters
written in granite
protruding over gentle hills.
One beside another,
and another, stones
that remind us you were here.

This is our defiant rainbow,
its broken stump still hidden
within the darkness of the storm.
Brother let me keep you company,
rub your tired feet. Let me
see you home.

The woman I will be
invites good friends to table.
Serves memory's food.
Tells stories
between the soup course
and her dream time.
Holds a granddaughter on her lap
and flies.

Hunger's table is unreachable in waiting,
its settings embrace discordant music,
noises that fill the head,
dishes bone clean and scraped,

a sound that courts the pain
of these brave times.

Welcome to our dear ghosts,
men whose historic flesh
plumps once-emaciated features,
who discreetly lift a saucer,
remarking upon its place and date
of fabrication.

Our brothers have forged
a terrible river.
Return has made them
more than hungry now.

The Staff of Life

Into the bottomless space his invasion left
back when your resistance took a turn
toward sublimation,
dissolve dry yeast in lukewarm water.
This sea throws up a tangle of passwords
on its beach.

Stir in honey, molasses, or brown sugar,
dry milk if milk is what you drink.
Add whole wheat flour and beat well
with a wooden spoon, 100 strokes.

No beating was necessary to seal your lips
back then, only the steel promise
of his gentleman's eyes.
Let rise until double in volume
and in meaning.
One day the rising of your rage
will dissolve the fear,
I promise you this.

But when you fold in salt and oil, your heart
may harden into rifts of terror.
By adding 2 cups white flour and
another wheat, you
slowly build the mass you need
to "get on with life."

It is wrongly your responsibility –to clean
his image with strong forearms,
kneading fingertips.
Slapping and gathering in the dough

is an exercise in pain control.
You have it now, have earned it

with a life remembered and cherished
as bread from the fire
calms this cusp of years.
We are always as strong
as our waiting need demands.

First rising 50 to 60 minutes,
second 40 to 50.
Between them make a fist and punch
the risen dough, but gently.
Remember, this is your food, not his face
flattened by dust and the sifting of time.

Shape loaves in greased pans
and let rise one last breath of air:
20 minutes to 1/2 hour will do.
Finally, brush with a wash
of cold water or milk and egg.
Then bake. 350 degrees
for 25 minutes or until golden brown.

Remove from pans and cool
or eat right away.
Eat right away.

Ingredients:

2 packages dry yeast dissolved in 3 cups lukewarm water
1/4 cup honey, molasses, or brown sugar
1 cup dry milk, optional
4 cups whole wheat flour
4 teaspoons salt
1/3 cup oil
2 cups unbleached white flour
1 cup whole wheat flour

Rice Pudding

If the mind stops
there is always rice pudding.
My father's Alzheimer's
was a word we never spoke.
It cradled our terror
like flame
ready to close the throat,
pull memory down to ash.

A handful of rice
and lots of water.
Nothing measured
demands your spent attention.
When he opened his mouth
the sentences would not line up,
refused
to hold their own.

I wondered
if there was a moment
beyond which nothing wept or strained
against the tide.
A stick of cinnamon,
curled about his hope.
After boiling to consistency–
a little sugar, perhaps some milk.

Rice pudding is
the ease with which you concede
the journey, nothing more
is up to you.

Nothing predictable.
To live without sure knowledge,
yes or no,
is my inheritance.

This and his years of love,
first home,
once living eyes
disappearing into a final cage of bone.

Exorcism

Two dark wings, heartbeat of feathers.
Or will it be a breast this time,
surgically cornered
to block the known caress?

A puzzle of words crosses your silence.
Breathing becomes a code.
Of ease, only random numbers
remain.

You must fix anchor to this beating
of anticipated days.
Follow the blood
fresh beets deposit on the knife.

Stained fingers
lift them from the cooking pot,
steal them from heat, bathe them
so that touch is possible.

Finger the skins
that shear beneath a steady stream.
Clean and slice.
Discard remaining grit

until the memory of their plumpness calls.
Neither armored nor worn
but futured in their perfect egos,
roots to be pared

as thin as the pages in this book of chance.
Add the translucence of onion,

white against wine.
Balsamic vinegar, a bit of oil and salt.

Each minute brings its story.
Each new fear this adventure of wings.

FROM

Where They Left You for Dead & Halfway Home

(Boulder: EdgeWork Books, 2002)

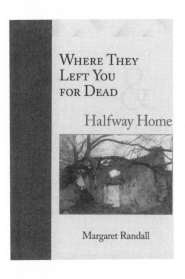

1

Last night
the whole countryside thrashed
in low grade fever

—Adrienne Rich

For the pain

I invent a gentler voice to greet your body, summon
touch to heal depleted earth. Memories of war
but faded. A childhood swallowed then spewed
in furious mouthfuls, the cardinal points
of imagery returned.

Barely visible line, moving from A to B, passing through
C. Curved taut as a bow, then gone. How to
find your way around the plateaus stenciled
on your back. We stumble, hurrying to overtake
a night sky.

Today a remedy looms. Then crouches again, folding
between your frozen eyes. Watchful. Tall but empty-handed.
Edges of scorched earth, peeling. Pain held
in increments, high-pitched, grieving only
its mirror self.

This is how I will say yes, still no sure answer
but absent of fear. You will hold moonlight-still,
waiting never your easiest strength. Something,
we agree, something unfamiliar. Coming
tomorrow.

3

I could slip anchor and wander
to the end of the jetty
uncoil into the waters
a vessel of light

—Audre Lorde

You say you are

leaving yourself behind. A sort of death (you watch
my face) but not in this dimension, a different recipe
for dying. Pay attention now. Watch your back,
both sides and everyone between: early family
requirements.

Forced to choose between this unnamed illness
and the labyrinth out, you must relax your gaze.
I cannot get close enough, cannot climb inside
your pummeled skin though I would barter
my years.

Helpless I follow your desperate gait, the streaks
of pain you trail. Climbing a debris field
of shifting boulders you despair, defy, break
running towards your infant self. Where they
left you for dead.

Now you pick life up and carry it. Life pokes
at this illness without name, crowds you, presses
for signature, forces a retake. You say you are
leaving yourself behind. I stand beside you,
waving.

12

telling myself stories
of someone I used to be

—Audre Lorde

You speak and I

listen. Words or silence, gesture or ribbon of sound
issuing from the punished cell, a door shutting
on memory that reemerges now to lift the chord
vibrating beneath this other
older pain.

As your body speaks I attend to signs, feel
for that hard knotting of tissue
where horror gathered its power to cripple and break.
Those who ask for proof have never tried to decipher
a body decoding.

Those who ask for proof have already taken sides.
In innocence or guilt they are complicit
with the damage done. She who loves this spirit
fighting to survive knows she must lick
raw wounds.

We invite the crime and criminal into our bedroom,
onto our bed. The flat of my palm fires up
each lump of fear, shares risk, dissolves,
an exercise in redemption circling back:
smoke-signal clear.

15

Men, once initiated, never get the
second chance . . . their loss, not
ours. Why borrow poverty?

—Ursula Le Guin

Montana, the monkey-faced spider

spins her web in the pale light of our front porch. From the
highest beam she descends along its orbed strands,
her larger shadow moving on the opposite wall, her work
a summer ritual that will end in the dying season
only to return with spring.

Then she will be another spider but we will
still call her Montana, watch her with the same intensity,
blessed she has chosen our entranceway
for her brief stay. Translucent body, resilient
and strong as steel.

In this house we are moving, have moved, will move
through that ancient rite: women becoming crones,
intoning the stories of our lives. Open to doors, eager
to learn the lessons however they are forged
in pain and change.

Even this unnamed illness, invisible to the experts,
a woman in movement, reflects Montana's natural style.
Birth of her home, death of a season, return of
her energies in a body new and ready once more
to enter its work of life.

19

. . . life escapes the broken clay of ourselves,
travels away from the center of our living."

—Linda Hogan

When I look from one perpendicular

canyon wall to another I always think of flying,
half-mile as the crow soars (here they are ravens,
blue-black wings in the highest branches of a tree).
I know the Anasazi tripped invisible hand-
and foot-holds

to mesa top, down to their homes in the caves
or into the narrow granaries. They couldn't have flown
(your eyes incredulous). You mean with wings? No, in their minds
I say, willing themselves from wall to wall, from canyon floor
to mountain ledge.

It is what I see. In the magical circle where Black Bear
rears straight up, in that furthest clearing where
a residue of fire still crowds to inches of our lives,
I imagine the wings of their thoughts, how they moved,
light as the movement of centuries.

If only your pain could fly, your body let go, unbend
in flight, I would coax the tightness from your limbs,
crack the stories of your other lives, offer
a perfect progression of notes, a gleaming sunrise
for your hair.

21

When I look into the mirror I see you . . .

—Pat Humphries and Judy Small

I write as you hurt

in these lines that leap from my drum-tensed skin
to the hungry page. In these poems you resist
asking only for bits of time, a place to let go
or remember with every weapon drawn.
I would give you healing

but in my proffered hands I only find another poem
and another, words where touch might have played
its curative part, my own relief where I
would gladly trade all hope for the fullness
of your body's gain.

My process born of your product, my release
sprung from your ache. If I could I would turn it
around, staunch this fierce spring so you
might stand and run and carry me with you
to whatever waits.

This minute you curl into text, deflate, expand,
a heart that beats the virtual reality of thunder
and response. You moan and I record the sound.
I tell and you reflect its fire in the coiled shadow
of unblinking eyes.

24

Things have a soul
and speak to us.

—Lorna Dee Cervantes

The robin who spoke to me

from a tree-branch, Mesa Verde, autumn of 1992, had money
on her mind. How will you divide it, store it (memories
of her stash of bugs), spend it, manage this most ominous
of tasks? A long question she answered without pause.
The language of robins

is bright as winter sun. It trips the edges of these canyons,
follows their snaked bodies into light, the call
of this valley we come back to, our hearts in empathy
with those who left their footprints here.
Softly robin spoke

and I listened. We took her advice and it served us well,
refining only details as we turn another corner
of our lives. Coffee can in the bedroom fills
with coins, counts itself out, offers a journey a year.
Caught in her magic

we cannot stay away. Money, not part of Anasazi life
is seamless in ours—if we recall the robin's chatter,
admonishment to love one another with the transparency
of land, drumming of cells, a burrowing trust
that calls us home.

27

We knew too much and
too little

—Marge Piercy

The past is

another country, people act differently there. Who
said that? No ready reference, nation or individual.
Wind bellows in the sheath between your muscles
and their housings, spins its erratic symphony
through my exhausted brain.

Present-tense of memory displays a legion of dolls
running in every direction. One turns her back
on the chorus, catches my eye as she whirls
colliding with other bodies of light, then pierces
the membranes of our century.

My mirror-image gathers momentum in its decision
to flee. Moves away inside itself. How we pad our nest
in a present struggling to keep its covenant
with that past. Somewhere a child cries for protection,
her need of sustenance, sleep.

The past is a country where no one speaks your name.
Still, wind lifts the pungent scent of silver roses
along its path. Recognition becomes a flame
flooding my eyes as I stroke the small of your
ever-vigilant back.

I live with circumstantial pessimism
and a fundamental historical optimism.

—Diana Kordon

Light is what floods me:

luminous cast of green filtering yellow violet red.
I escape into sea or sky, gain depth or altitude,
arms flapping. A long sail of full-lunged breath
and no one follows. When they trap freedom they will
bring me back

and just as calmly I will return to die. Successive nights,
repetitions parading the dream, machine-gun sweep of stars.
Flash to an old film: Jason Robards permitted to choose
the music that accompanies his death, settled on a pallet,
conveyor moving him from sight

into the mouth of science fiction movie-speak then spewed
as small green pellets, food for an over-peopled world.
Because it no longer frightens me I do not call this
nightmare. Because it assaults me night after night
I call it death.

But death of what? Hands flying wordlessly around a clock,
work that stumbles, impatience with men who lick
and close the envelope. This place where evil
is given other names so it may shame its way
to victory.

FROM

Halfway Home

(Boulder: EdgeWork Books, 2002)

The body embraces

its changing landscape grudgingly. Gives up
fighting pounds, limp hair, bleeding gums,
skin sagging into its web
or map of lines. Tired muscles
that refuse to pull the belly in, breasts up.
Okay, I say: you win. Garden of white silk
sprouting across my chin, at last
I welcome you to this new self-image,
understand—after all those hopeful dollars—
no glib promises will erase a beard
at odds with every presumption of beauty.

In a different world those dollars would feed
dozens of starving children, soothe
their skin—home to raw hunger—instead
of making promises they knew they
could not keep. Mine might have bought me
the Greek Isles or Alaska's Inside Passage.
Who knew? We were educated
not to know.

Today I say: come here white beard,
let me stroke your silvery hairs.
Take a break, tired abs, relax.
There are other jobs to be done,
deeper visions to sustain. The children
still starve. The liars will keep on smiling
until we meet them eye for eye,
stare their beckoning fingers down,
turn our backs on the insatiable demon

of regret
and stand with these body parts
that have served us long and well. With
liberty and justice for all. Amen.

Angelita, little angel

stoops beneath the weight of the smaller angel
riding on her back. Baby brother, four years
younger than she, curled in the frayed cloth
of her *rebozo*, smelling of fresh cornmeal
and dried urine, moving in unison
with his sister who walks her territory
on this Mexico City street: broad sidewalk
not quite to the corner where her fiefdom ends
and another child's begins. Back and forth,
slowly, squatting from time to time
against the great wall of Aztec stone,
ancestral temple now Ministry of Public Works
in a country where little angels are
as common as the scent of fresh *tortillas*
and modern tourist buses lumbering
through ancient streets. Angelita's eyes
and mouth, eyes and mouth
not nine but sixty-nine,
hold stories we cannot know.
Age lives in the eye of the beholder, in the
repetition of hungers, resignations,
and this terrible undying hope.

What fails

or ceases unfolds like a succession of trail rims.
Walking to the edge is not the same
as falling. More like drifting, but then remembrance
does not accompany the act.
I do not know, today, how flight will look
or feel. Conjecture: inadequate as rosebuds
not yet unfurled or wilting into disarray.
Only the moment of full bloom
embraces the whole picture.
Standing on the edge is merely standing
on the edge.
Having fallen, there is no memory
of past imaginings.
And this is a metaphor for every day
from here on out.

Patience pulls her long skirts

three-hundred-sixty degrees about her ankles
and squats before me on the floor.
Do I detect self-satisfaction in her gaze?
Her balance brings me back
to my Vietnamese sisters down Highway One
to Quang Tri, 1974. Rocking gently
on their heels, comfortable, serene.

Patience has come to stay.
She occupies her place, looks up at me
—no need for words—intention perfectly clear.
We never got along that well before.
Was it me? Was it too soon?
Years ago I could have used her wise demeanor
when schoolgirl rituals kept me at the edge of life.

Her presence might have softened the falls
with one man after another.
And in 1989, when the world came apart
her embrace might have helped me through.
Sorry, she says, didn't you know
I am blood of your blood flesh of your flesh?
Still, I only sit with those
who have paid their dues in years.

The unburied, the missing

come back to me now. Roque, months older than I
when we started out, forever forty.
Doris María, who would not become a teen.
The plane that took her falls from the sky,
falls again each time I turn my eyes to hers:
round in their fear of fire. Nothing will happen next.
María Otilia Vargas, 75-year-old retired teacher,
widow of Osvaldo Pérez, mother of
Dagoberto, Aldo, Carlos, Iván, Mireya and Patricia,
the first gunned down in a fire-fight against the dictator,
next two extinguished in that long war's torture cells
and the twins still missing, "disappeared"
in that language of Chilean pain. Only Patricia
lives, one year unraveling into the next,
accompanying her mother's purpose
in sweet madness. Together they study each release
on a list published all these years too late.
Their beloved names aren't there,
yet the mother continues to tempt them
with rice pudding,
shelter their bodies from the night air,
cradle them against her hopeful breast.
Otilia, condemned
to live these years her children could not have.
Even Patricia has lost count: the sister and brothers
torn from her childhood murmur in her ear.
The missing will only come back to eat with us
when we set a table
served with the food of change.

for Otilia Vargas, compañera

These years have carved

deep questions in my mouth.
Would I be this woman
without that dark spit of a country road
up from the border with Guatemala,
fragility riding in the back seat
of my car?

Even the faded late-night argument
—does god exist?—
on my high school prom night.
Couples around us necking
(that's what we called it then)

but my date and I, scrubbed adolescents,
one would grow up to be a preacher,
ping-ponged for hours,
our passion filling the night,
red rock warm beneath the tulle of my dress,
sun beginning to light the Jémez sky.

Surely my long-dead painter friend
helped point me in this direction,
her generous length of newsprint
torn in magnificent gesture
as she commanded: draw!
Don't be afraid to ruin a length

or many lengths. Go on, try.
And the brushes she bought
were always the best, insisting
I would only know if I loved the craft
after using the master's tools.

Years later the poet told us
the master's tools
can never be used
to dismantle the master's house:
words that took up residence
in my focus and my hand.

I Ching tells us writing
cannot express words completely
nor words completely express thoughts.
The woman I am reflects
these moments living in my cells,

some strain against
a traveled road of growth.
Others offer a hand,
invite me to revisit places
inhabited too briefly, departed
without saying goodbye.

From this highpoint on the trail
the city below is a toy,
but I have recorded its harmony,
embraced its distance, glimpsed
the semblance of its yearning face.

Three years

and no poems came. I thought
it might be about transition
from one sort of work to another,
what we call retirement
because our language
has no other word by which to measure
that change of seasons.

Maybe it's this struggle to publish,
I said, nobody interested these days
in what I need to say.
You urged: be easy with yourself,
there's time to rest and read
and know that you are safe.

I rested and read
and knew I was safe.
Still the poems did not come.
Do I call myself poet, I asked,
may I continue to claim
the honor of the cloth, its warrior name?

And then, one day, a woman
whose history held hands with mine
stopped me mid-sentence.
You will not write again, she said,
until you can grieve the utopia,
peel away the adjectives,
make peace with the loss.

We dance to the slow tunes now,
poetry and I.

Finding an easy stride

I walk this trail I have walked
so many times before,
plant my feet as I climb, leaning
slightly forward on the descent,
your gift of moving light.

Its rhythm pulls me up, lures me
into canyons where water is marked
by stands of yellowing cottonwoods,
coyote scat deep purple
along the narrowing path.

I stand. Silent. Only
the measure of my breath
unnerves this bright blue butterfly
whose flight becomes an avalanche
on distant mountain slopes.

I stoop to hold the small stone
my eye discovers
just before it lodges in my heart.
Polished amber. Watermelon-flecked.

Turning the trophy in my hand
a curtain parts
and I know when I raise my eyes
memory will swirl about my head,
the faces of those who have gone
will turn towards mine,

their voices muted, stories complete,
nothing but honor in their eyes.

Last Poem

At least for now.

I too make love and talk about it later,
said the poet.

Each time she speaks she reinvents herself,
gives birth to the intimate details:
courage to some, scandal to others.

To save her life
the writer had to depart the battlefield.
Still, she fights with every sinew and breath
believing she can change her world.

Although they accuse her of deviancy, poetry,
stridency or the bliss of ignorance,
hers is the possible hunger,
the unbroken sequence of choice.

FROM

Into Another Time: Grand Canyon Reflections

(Albuquerque: West End Press, 2004)

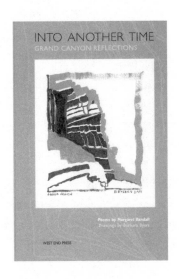

Great Unconformity

Walls of black and rust, orange
and red, delicate creamy pink
and every tone of brown,
green and blue and sudden yellow.
Each purple hue and living shape,
sculpts bowls, ebbs and returns,
laps a sheen polished by the power,
millennia of water.
Steadfast schist shot through by pink arrows
straight as my searching gaze.

Yet unconformities, missing chapters
of geologic record
occur when erosion removes a layer of rock
between eons of slow formation.
Grand Canyon gives us
one Great Unconformity
and the Greatest Angular Unconformity:
dramatic examples of this process.

The Canyon as we experience it today
began to form between 1 and 1.8 billion years ago:
close approximation by geology's clock.
Sand and mud accumulated to an unknown thickness,
heat and pressure later turning these
to Vishnu Schist, gneiss, and Zoroaster Granite:
names assigned by modern scribes,
processes we imagine
drawing on every supposition of scale and light.

Between 1.8 and 1.2 billion years ago
the earlier formations became high mountains
intruded by thin white dikes of coarse pegmatite
and thick pink granite.
Between 1.2 billion and 900 million years ago
deposits of late Proterozoic sediments
sat on the eroded knees of mountains.

This is the Greatest Angular Unconformity,
something no longer there,
no longer quantifiable
or possible to assess.
Something we imagine
or cannot begin to imagine.
Not unlike the words *portage* or *decibel*:
absent hours from my speech.

Eight hundred million years ago
tilting and faulting changed the sedimentary layers
into another series of mountains and valleys.
No one alive
can be sure how those rises and depressions
really looked. No tactile animal sense
or human talent
welcomes their contours
through eyes, pores, touch of impatient feet.
Five hundred seventy million years ago
new erosion produced a flat lowland plain
and the first invasion of Paleozoic seas.

What sat and soared
created the Great Unconformity
winking at us now

between the chunky comfort of Tapeats Sandstone
and the Chuar Group: Kwagunt, Galeros and Nankoweap.
Somewhere around 245 million years ago
325 million years of Paleozoic Era
painted the sediment
now fixed upon our eyes.

During this period another lesser unconformity
appeared like a word misspelled,
a letter missing
from the practiced lexicon of life.
My life. How it falters. A slip here,
scratch there.
Reaching for balance, clawing at certainty.
The surface of something, altered.
The moment it takes to assimilate this new place
on the body's map,
unsure it will be there when I look again.

Two thousand feet of sediment rose
during the Mesozoic Era 70 million years ago.
All these dinosaur-age deposits
would later erode
except for the whisper
where we enter this river.
The dinosaurs themselves
occupy our memory,
placed by those who shoot their consumer product
into our consciousness.

From 70 to 40 million years ago
what we call the Colorado Plateau
began to rise
and Grand Canyon as we know it

initiated its relentless journey
into sight and taste and need.
Modern Grand Canyon: 5 to 1 million years young:
its Coconino and Esplanade Sandstone
Redwall and unconsolidated dolomites
Muav Limestone and Bright Angel Shale.

A vertical mile below its rim
we invite time and pre-human history
into our hungry bodies,
open our hands, bare our teeth, call out
in a voice too pale
too small too reticent
when faced with the power of mortality
perfectly balanced upon opposing rocks.

At any moment the frustration of a word
forgotten in Spokane,
a woman in Albuquerque moving to place her hand
on the small of her lover's back,
a baby elephant in Tanzania
slipping beneath its mother's swaying belly,
a burst of swallows
lifting off Managua's astonished streets,
the movement of eagerness, hope or critical acclaim
sends a rockslide of change
into the arms of that river.
Altering its shape. Pushing it into tomorrow.

I fix the age to come
beside my moment of witness,
simple cry for help.
Words—forgotten and found—
sift between my teeth,

fall about me
rising and reaching,
freeing both knowledge and doubt,
places I will visit next, click of ideas
settling into the slots
created by my own unconformity:
this passage to next year,
a welcome harbinger of relief.

It All Stops Here

It all stops here:
the ravished self
battered by truncated thought
and misplaced words,
bones threatening to crack
beneath the pressure
of reaching and pulling,
concern for that space
beyond the envelope
or inside the envelope.
The withering fears
and everyday dilemmas.

Here shear walls take over,
pulling me skyward.
The sky itself
narrows to a strip
between their towering heights,
presents night's velvet
studded by distant worlds,
each drawing me
washed and gentled
into its mindless orb.

Here I am concerned
with staying in the boat
as it gives itself
to Kanab's long wave train,
with perfectly framing
the image that claims my heart
or finding a cool spot
to camp along the hot sand beach,

careful to leave no trace
on earth that will host another
when I depart,
bestowing nothing but footprints
and gratitude.

Freeway traffic backed up
for twenty miles,
impossible telephone menus
when all I need is a human voice,
automatons, their arms raised
to position the ringing cell phone,
overkill of noise and filth
claiming the food I eat,
the air I struggle to breath.
All this recedes from me now.

I sit on a heft of driftwood
tossed to this beach
one or one hundred years ago,
allow nerve-endings
to follow half-closed eyes
down river
into another time.
For it is time
that carries us here
more purposefully than space:
non-linear time
coiling to fill the jagged holes
our system's latest consumer demand
leaves in its corrosive wake.

The Notebook

1

I brought a notebook,
carefully chosen with just the right feel,
a pleasing relationship
between its sturdy cover
and unlined pages.

I wanted heavy paper,
a spiral binding
to withstand the river's wear and tear,
necessary flexibility
when—I imagined—
I would sit on low rocks,
balancing these writing materials
across my swollen knees.

Pen-Tab Industries
produced this particular writer's tool,
100 sheets of 20-pound paper
between cover stock of at least 150 weight,
7 x 5 inches the outer measurement
that allows my book
to slide easily into a zip-lock bag
where a selection of pens
also resist a breach of water.

On my notebook's plain black cover
a seal with the trademark EXPERT
is embossed in gold.
Beside it I added an elegant sticker
proclaiming "Girls Kick Ass"

that one of our guides passed out one day,
imbuing my book
with just the appropriate quota
of belligerence and pride.

2

I came home
with my notebook empty.
Not a line. Not a word.
Not a quote or point of interest
written to aid my failing memory.
Neither did I make a single mark
in the river guide
kept safe and dry
in the same plastic bag.

Not a sketch.
Not the name of a companion river-runner
nor the number of cubic feet per second
this season's water runs.
No reference to the millions or billions of years
it took to raise these rock walls
above my awe-struck eyes.

The writer wrote nothing:
neither random thought
nor carefully copied statistic,
river story nor important date,
geologic event or human accomplishment.

Each time there was a choice
between writing or silently sitting,
inhaling this place,

letting it enter my pores,
I chose to open myself,
invite the place in.
Did I know then
I would be able to access it later?
I didn't even ask the question.

A book of blank pages:
the better to see, feel, absorb
that wordless energy
embracing my shoulders,
the sharp pain knotted in my throat
or drumming at my temples
exploding all givens
and spinning me into that place
where I see with new eyes,
hear with freshly-opened ears,
tell the story in a language
that brings the experience back to life.

Numbers wriggle and sweat
in any description of this place.
Scientific names,
geological conclusions,
the suppositions of anthropologists
bear only partial witness.

Rejecting the known language
I begin to create
the one I need in which to keen and shout.

Silence

In the thundering roar of water,
in the dry up-canyon winds
hissing between these stoic walls,
in the long crescendo of frog song, cicada,
a thousand pair of beating wings
and the songs of other resident creatures,
silence settles
deep as memory.

The electric whir of every known appliance
rumble of cities and even towns,
cough of revving motors, din of traffic,
phones ringing, hawkers invading
the boundaries of our senses,
their cacophony blurred
into one unending decibel—
all are absent here.

Nestled against the backdrop
of that natural symphony:
only the beating of your heart,
only mine.

FROM

Stones Witness

(Tucson: University of Arizona Press, 2007)

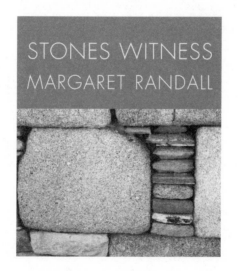

Time

1

At the edge of my city
fingers brush the incised circle
still visible on cliffs
of cured basalt.
Depiction of sun, moon, year.
Opening to another world
or to the body,
power perhaps, or the beginning.
Beginning as in
any point along a circle.

Soon a road
will blaspheme this land
where twelve hundred years ago
our ancestors
chipped these images
on fallen rock.
Evidence
of what was experienced, thought, known
returning persistent questions.

2

At Chaco's northernmost reach
two towers,
each catching moonrise
in the perfect balance
of its slender notch.
Astronomical alignments

speaking to future.
Once every 18.6 years
the lunar standstill
cycles from Pueblo Bonito's priests
to our forced double take.

3

At Kiet Seel
we find no timepieces
among ceramic shards,
no minute or second hands,
no Calendar Stone
adorns the kiva
or elsewhere in this alcove
where bits of yucca rope
wait to be retrieved
by hands that weave and knot,
tie turkey feathers
fix handles to obsidian blades.

Without time
does timelessness exist?
Recent, yes, and long ago.
When we were young
or yesterday
but never five minutes from now.
Seasons and moons,
growth and hungers
pronounce these meanings
we fashion to such accurate degree.

No steady ticking clock
to guide all other clocks.

No ringing of bells
at any hour.
No Greenwich Mean, no zones
unfolding as they circle
a planet now known to be round.
No tomorrow
unfurling before today.
Only a time of cold. A time of rain.
A time of balm
against your ready skin.

4

It wouldn't have been
our ten in the morning,
birthday or anniversary.
Noon yes, sun directly above,
dusk or dawn as signifiers,
seasons to plant and reap,
days not weighted
by these divisions
we use to punish or reward.

Today we walk with pedometer,
work
where we privilege accuracy,
time management, date book.
No acknowledgment of limits
unfettered by resting heart rate.
No measure but taste.
Life surely more
than this arbitrated passage
killing as it goes.

5

Rhythmic drip from the spring
at the back of the cave,
its punctual sound accompanying
heartbeat and footstep
as it layers or peels away
the cache of memory
inhabiting hand and breast.

Show me dimension:
linear, circular
or beyond a known direction.
Show me
where count met breath for you.
I know your working hands
saw future,
understood this mirror
traveling from my time to yours,
asking the questions
cluttering my mouth.

6

When the last family
let the great log fall
between stone walls
across entrance or exit,
when this place was abandoned
in—now we can reckon it—1286
the only date was a place
no longer bountiful,
the need to find home
somewhere else.

Time spills through my hands,
the beating of a great heart
slow as consciousness
quickened only
by this fitful memory
coiling in my throat,
reaching my mouth,
jolting my pulse
to recognition.

Breaking Open Like a Rock

for Sebastián Pérez Mondragón
born January 26, 2002

Emerging. Forgetting. Forgetting
as he emerges,
a child struggles through the birth canal
passing himself on the way out.
He sheds memory as rock sheds light
when desert brings night down
about its shoulders.

Sebastián, your ancient mask
trails secrets
dimmed by this new consciousness
we thrust upon you,
eyes follow your mother's hand,
leave dimensions no longer only yours:
time's curve, the temperature of stars.

Necessary trade-off, unidirectional,
its reward this migration
from place to place,
this wind turned heat,
this joy subdued in quick fix
—trapping as it fabricates
our need.

Sebastián, in your drawn cheeks
and perfect mouth
I trace what you once knew,
heights and valleys, germinating sound.

Memory releases you now
as you reach to grasp the lifeline
we anchor and hold out.

One day when we stop our obscene wars
in a thirsty season
watered by sudden desert rain,
your lost memory will spring to life
and we will gather at your feet.

Will you be the one
who teaches us to read our world
from center out
or will we swallow you whole
like those others
who fell from that once-secure place,
breaking open like a rock
to place their secrets in our eyes?

Ferry to the Other Side

Borders lean into my eyes, their cobalt towers
word and stone, their shimmer fading
to grain.
Words thrown by giant hands
attached to arms on bodies like my own.
But the stones,
the stones stand together, immense and perfect,
not a knife blade parting their seamless joints,
not a trickle of salt.

A border of language follows me home,
each journey a plea for forgiveness,
jutting cliff and long way down.
We manage translation like trade.
You take this, I that,
while the crow, motionless on its fragile branch,
holds me in its eye.

Straddling borders I birthed four children
cut from the substance of language
while I waited,
words piling in my throat.
Four children cradled
between the there and now of dreams.

One bridged convention, a vow of nations
placing the scales of Justice in his hands.
Second raced to catch up,
looked quickly in both directions,
weaving a holding pattern
about insistent turns.

Third stared straight ahead,
her dark eyes testing the clarity of waters.
And last embraces seasons,
dresses in honey hues, calling her shots
from the ledges of tall buildings.

My borders run in their veins,
rivers of denial, candy kisses
wary and bittersweet.
In time their children
will discover the fields of longing
hidden in the ravine between my sagging breasts.

Generations crossing borders,
bridges not yet imagined
beneath a rain of paper airplanes.

Twins

1

"Women?" I ask, "men, or maybe neither?"

"Neither," you agree—after a short silence—and I understand
you are not denying them gender, only saying that gender seems
irrelevant considering the length of their journey.

2

In the simple clutter of Amman's small archeological museum we
stand before a modest glass case. The descriptive label reads "Twins,
6,500 BC." In smaller print there is something about this being
the first known sculpture. Meaning, I know, the first unearthed by
curious hands, for us to question, contemplate.

Neolithic humans, possessing neither arms nor legs, take our hands
and whisper, "Follow me."

A single squared and armless torso supports two long necks, one
beside the other, each topped by a fine-featured face. A repetition
of small mouths, delicate noses, and wide-set eyes stare back at the
viewer, simultaneously gifting and asking. The eyes are rimmed in
heavy black: ancient mascara or simple definition.

Three feet tall by half as broad, the twinned figure modeled in rich
brown clay seems low-fired though hardy enough to have withstood
millennia. Smooth areas are over-patched with rough.

The face to the right (the viewer's left) is slightly more settled than
its twin; the face on the left more intense. Both sets of eyes pierce

museum glass, cultural and emotional barriers, all possible degrees of separation.

3

Despite the absence of breasts or breadth of life-bearing hips, despite there being no visual sexual clue, I see the single-bodied figures as female. Woman is writ large to me—in the dual gaze, shape of facial features, angle of necks, resignation and fragility of shoulders. Sisters stand before me, complicit, staring back through eight-and-a-half millennia. The only language we need is one of gesture, acknowledgment.

Who were these twins, in their lives and in the intention of the artist who fashioned them? Real twins—conjoined or not—duality in a single being, lovers or kindred spirits, siblings or a statement of relationship against all threat?

Who shaped this clay, modeled these features, and why? Are we to experience conversation here?
Familiarity?
Monumentality?
Intimate recognition?

4

Such difference
in a single body,
such unity before a world
where complexity fractures
light years beyond the Morning Star.

Such fierce devotion to self
piercing me with
                        their/her
gaze, embracing me
armless, bringing me
into the burning circle of
their/her
            presence,
a gaze that stops us where we stand,
turns us gently, deftly,
and points us
toward our own beginnings.

Canyon del Muerto

for Jules and Karen

1

No sound but the lives
of those who went before
wind in orchards of peach and apple,
sound of opuntia and willow,
ripple of grama grass and jimsonweed
fancy-dancing in their eyes.

Cottonwood silence, great branches
reaching to hold you,
white sun rimming their thick bark.
Golden eagle silence, nighthawk
and cliff swallow silence, great horned owl
sitting and staring eye to eye.

Sound of coyote running, watching
black bear and bobcat,
porcupine, badger, elk and mule deer
foraging, roaming these whispering canyons.
Wild turkey offering his feathers,
keeping you warm and safe.

Hunter-gatherers
until a knowledge of corn
traveled north from Mexico
along with abalone shells,
seeds and feathers
more brilliant than any they'd seen.

Silence of the terrified
trapped by Spanish bullets at Massacre Cave
(unheard by Narbona's severed ears).
Sound of U.S. cavalry bullets
forcing the people to Bosque Redondo.
Sound of silence, of tears, of waiting.

Deer-hoof rattle and bone flute,
games of chance, seeds and stones.
Sound of hot stones
dropped one by one
into water-tight baskets
until their heat made cooking possible.

No sound now but water rushing,
tumbling over the stones of Chinle Wash
seeping slowly, lowering the level
of *tinajas* in slickrock,
rush of falls carrying river
along this valley floor.

Sound of our breathing
in this place where nothing stirs
but mountain lion and cottontail,
snakeweed and yucca
sagebrush and juniper
in blinking patchwork,
shifting light.

Sheep bells and barking dogs
ten thousand years to now
Archaic, Basketmaker, Ancestral Puebloan, Pueblo
(names we give them),
Hopi and Dineh (names they give themselves),
all at home on this canyon floor.

Crumbling rock walls and cedar beams
fading to stone hogans, barbed-wire fences
moving through measurements
that refuse to enter our notion of hours or miles
but wait around the bend or here in the hollow
where one long shadow casts its meaning over rock.

2

Down Pine Tree Trail we stumble
on rain-chewed earth, cross clay mulch
fevered to our touch.
Descending from wind-swept rim
drawings chipped and paled by time
the work of ancestor artists.

My breath tightens at the cave
remembering the single woman who hid
beneath her dead companions
until next day's light
and the people who watched
in helpless quiet across that wounded space.

Their stories as different
from the soldiers' stories
as the eyes of the Iraqi child,
recording her last image of invaders,
are from their weapons trained on her childness,
the explosion that ends her life.

Across the river and up another fragile bank
our packs come off,
we crawl beneath barbed-wire strands,

go on once more
to continue this pilgrimage
to a people whose home is a silence filled with sound.

A people who invite us in,
great-grandchildren of their murderers
descending these canyon walls
by ladders of grief
and gratitude
one brilliant day in March.

Then up again,
switchbacks of timber and stone
carved into a path they call Twin Trail
to the low-slung woods and dirt roads
dotted with trailers and pickups:
life as it sounds today.

Changing of the Guard

Twentieth-century woman stubs her toe
on twenty-first century rock—
explosion in an empty room.
It wasn't there a moment ago
or anywhere in her trailing past.
She didn't expect its stubborn bulk,
the crooked bone, the pain.

Twentieth-century woman
can't find the switch, remembers
only a sliver of used light.
Noise too much, too loud.
Air too thick.
She turns her eyes to the throb of faces
crowding her once-familiar path,
getting in her way.

Twentieth-century woman holds hands
with time, grabs its fingers,
won't let go.
She cannot look back
or touch the box
she must make sure
stays tightly shut.

Time, always time
spilling across the interface
dividing her century from this,
telling her sound-bites
sound-bites swift as darts
moving too fast about her,

entering her secret places,
knocking her down.

When she tries to get up
the moment is gone.
Sand fills her eyes. Nothing is green.
No audience waits in the cavernous hall,
no performers on stage,
no end game
to help revive her breath.

Throwing My Voice to Weather

This poem
throws my voice to weather,
pulses a room
or pulls dark shrouds
about your trembling shoulders,
shifts weight from body
to silhouette
against the broken wall.

Speech American as apple pie
or belligerent identity:
the Jewish girl
who fashioned her culture
from small flags, stolen passports,
nacatamales and the blood red
of ancient armless figures:
a sky too big for trouble.

When I am gone
my voice will look for me
in narrow canyons,
shallow river caves,
the peregrine's nest
abandoned this season
but feverish
in its remembrance of tiny beaks.

Battered by age and cluttered,
ragged catch in the throat,
warble or whine

where full-timbered words
once took flight,
my voice completes the cycle now
moves into an uplift
of memory.

Will it emerge
with a child's questions on its tongue
or full-toned and powerful,
ready for battle again?

Corner of Latin America

La esquina de Latinoamérica
it's called
where a weathered fence of rusted metal
cuts white sand, then disappears
into water that has no knowledge
of borders.

Metal recycled
from Vietnam-era tanks and planes,
gap-toothed and bearing improbable image
of cactus and skeleton.
Broken pilings, a division
that once was: what? Shabby, imposing,
makeshift, or absurd bravado?

This corner of Latin America,
where lines on a map
translate to searchlights, guns,
pickup beds heavy with hunched men and women
caught, taken back to their point of origin
only to try again tomorrow
or next week.

Corner, as in the uppermost and outermost
point on a map
once inhabited by Kiet Seel to the north
Casas Grandes to the south.
Not a place that gathers,
enfolds, comforts or protects.
Not refuge but exposure.
Danger writ large in global script.

One side of the worn fence
a young man lifts his body in push-ups,
strains against twisted pieces
of a cement platform, crumbling.
Woman and child
sleep in the fence's long shadow.
Far side: San Diego's powerful skyline
disappearing in mist.

La esquina de Latinoamérica,
containment vs. we don't want you—
except to watch our children, clean
our floors, keep our profit high.
Like a hologram, this place
emptied of itself,
waits restive for change.

In dreams and in grief
I am riding that corner fence,
its rusted metal cuts the flesh
of my thighs.
Blood runs to the sand
then disappears
as high tide takes the beach.

Margaret in 2008.
At Naropa University, Boulder, Colorado.

FROM

Their Backs to the Sea

(San Antonio: Wings Press, 2009)

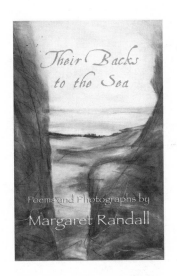

Island Without a Name

The universe is built like an enormous feedback loop,
a loop in which we contribute to the ongoing creation
of not just the present and the future but the past as
well.

—John Wheeler

1

Your tongue swells, its smallest gland
still secretes saliva, lining your mouth
with precious wetness.
Lifetime of days brave oppositional winds,
waves overpowering dual hulls
bound together in defiance
of currents, rain and scorching sun.

Southern Cross imprinted upon
unflinching sky.
Searching eyes follow sun's arc
and lunar calendar traces your course
across, against, and down wind
toward destination
or surprise.

Sea turtle swims, raising her small head
above the rolling surf.
Later you will peck her image in rock
framed by a ring of smaller stones.
She will be cicerone and teacher,
nourish hunger
and the patience of song.

Without compass or other nautical device
dolphins and circling land birds
guided your earliest settlers in.
You say Hotu Matu'a was the first
landing at Anakena with his wife, six sons
and extended family, origin of your lineage
in the stories you remember.

Unyielding Pacific, 1,300 miles west of Chile,
1,260 southeast of Pitcairn,
at 27 point 9 south and 109 point 26 west
in the measurements we use today,
a journey of stars beckoned you then,
exhausted but ready,
to this speck of land.

2

Why did you leave the pungent bounty
of Marquesas, Mangareva, Pitcairn
or Henderson
for this hard triangle
lost in the lonely waters of south central Pacific,
its coast repelling every landing
but one, almost every stretch

of rocky shore menacing, threatening
rather than welcoming
your arrival? Relentless
you struggled ashore, opened your eyes
on this slip of lava: ash and obsidian
anchored by three volcanoes
promising balm to your thirst.

When did you come? Some say 1,200 AD,
others earlier, surely before 800
of our era—an era
that would invade you centuries later
in the crazed imposition of men
bearing crosses, determined to break
your hearts and minds: suffocation of conquest.

3

Sixteen million palms once stood upon this mound
of rocky soil. Rope from the bark
of *hau hau* trees and others whose wood
was good for sea-going craft.
Forest, but only a single intermittent stream,
no river to relieve your thirst: cane juice
rotting your teeth as it kept you alive.

Offshore, bubbling up from saltwater depths
and dangerous rock
a freshwater spring still caresses cracked tongues.
The marshy lakes in the craters
of *Rano Kau, Rano Aroi* and *Rano Raraku*
comfort parched cells,
nourish you still.

Weather was always here: winds attacking
from every direction: above, below,
east, south, west, north. Until the palms
were gone, leaving only their memory.
No more canoes. Twisted paper mulberry
offering only beaten cloth
and mirror-image carvings.

Tides and fevers brought on the nausea
of vertigo: whipping your bodies,
pulling you
from the pleated crests
of ridges squeezed in giant fists,
released when tsunamis sucked
the hissing sea from shore.

4

Little grew in that shallow soil: sweet potatoes,
yams, taro, guava, sugar, and plantains
in lava-tube caves.
Chicken and vegetables. Fish and seabirds.
Sailing vessels brought Polynesian, then Norwegian rats:
—the shameful delicacy. And much later
sheep: tens of thousands, but not for you.

As if leeching life from rock was not enough
to set family upon family, call forth
survival wars, a taste for human flesh
and successive battles, other arrivals
brought animals not for your sustenance,
languages not for your lips, new rules
that pinned you to careening history.

5

In 1722 a Dutch admiral may have been the first
to spot your presence, gaze in astonishment
at the guardians standing sentinel
along your shores. His logbook said Easter
and he bestowed the Christian name.

You say *Tê Pito o te Henua*: navel
of the world. Rapa Nui.

Later English, French, Germans, Russians,
Chileans, and North Americans
found you, stayed hours or days
before giving up on your loneliness,
carried news of those statues,
their backs to the sea their stoic faces
watching over fields and boat-shaped homes.

In 1862 Peruvian slavers kidnapped 1,500
of your healthiest men
and when protest forced them to return
a single starving boatload, the dozen survivors
brought smallpox and tuberculosis,
reducing your population
to a struggling hundred and ten.

Lay brother Eugene Eyraud stayed years
dogged in his sacrifice, obsessive
to convert, to remake you
in the image of his suffering.
He died content he'd saved every island soul
while you made the sign of the cross
and hid your gods for all to see.

6

Thus the vast sheep station with 70,000 head.
Thus their fences and your taking:
tradition of dreaming what was needed,
announcing you were coming to get it
and making good on your promise,

but always leaving enough
so your oppressors would not starve.

Assaulting your island again and yet again,
pushing you into a crowded corner:
La compañía explotadora de la Isla de Pascua
—company to exploit the island—
with its history of debt enslavement,
rules imposed by those whose god
still signals plunder and abuse.

Memory stretched by long-range voyaging
you lost the wood for your canoes,
lost the traditional skills
for those explorations of blood
and spirit, but still greeted
the whalers and schooners and steamers
that would change your destiny.

7

Despite repression, hardship, hunger
and disease,
you gave birth and flourished,
new life opening against the odds.
Neither ravages of foreign invasion
nor cousin blood
could erase you from this place.

Those who arrived and looked and fled,
invented stories for the world:
reverse migrations to fit poor theory:
Inca travelers, aliens from outer space,
Lemuria's lost continent

or a Third Race of Giants
appearing, disappearing, then rising again.

Later some came with open-ended questions:
Mrs. Routledge on her *Mana,* Metraux, Mulloy,
even Heyerdahl who worked so hard
to prove his forced hypothesis.
What was proven possible did not happen,
and as discovery turns
so turn the disappearing pages
of an ancient book

what emerges is this: we cannot unravel
your lost world
without having lived its life, faced the wind
and knelt to chip away
at volcanic tuff turning mountains to men
then moving the magical tonnage miles
to stand in silence, backs to the sea.

We must suffer like you, need like you,
lose what you lost
and hold what you held.
Think like you, bargain
the same solutions to the same problems.
In our lives' safe otherness
there is no imagining yours.

8

Questions bulk against the windswept slopes
of grassy hills and dark cliffs.
How did you nourish yourself
with scant rain, thin soil, no coral reef

and few fish, how reconcile yourself
to no more wood, no escape
from 63 square miles lost in the desolate Pacific.

You answer with closed fists
hidden behind your backs,
steadfast gaze focused on goals
that evoke descriptions
such as *childlike* or *trickster*,
as you who remember those who remember
stutter and die.

Isolation and contact: adversarial extremes
of an ongoing argument,
what you made and used
thousands of miles from easier lands
and what you brought with you
when you came, pushing adaptation
one generation to the next.

9

The *moai*: 288 laying where—thrown
       from their *ahu:* stone bases
that served as drying platforms for the dead
then tombs for their bones—they follow
stone's cycle into earth. Almost 400
still stand in the quarry
at *Rano Raraku,* or on its outer flank

amidst picks and hammers, cutting and shaping tools:
implements of an art that stopped one day
as if the artists suddenly departed
those great cavities of negative space,

length of a body here, dismembered head
beyond. I scramble across a nose
discovering it is a nose.

Two hundred and two remain in transit,
their unfinished journey through wind
and light. Eight hundred eighty seven
in all: emerging
through stone birthing canals,
kneeling, walking, standing tall
or gone to recovering earth.

Their eyes—sockets pulling us into vacancy—
are silent now beneath broad overhang
of brow. Some once held eyeballs:
coral, obsidian, red scoria
inserted and then removed,
unleashing or retrieving
mana for those who believed.

Too many outsiders took the sacred relics,
leaving nothing but trinkets
and disease.
Those who learned the language
received some stories
but most discarded your people's memory
in favor of their own.

10

Kohau rongorongo's talking wood
left us rows of tiny characters,
shark-bone incisions on small boards:
a script not yet deciphered

by your descendants
though some recite clan boundaries
or broken genealogies.

Notes meant to invoke memory
and ideas that are key,
not letter for letter, word for word.
Those who insist on looking
for the clues that brought
other ancient scripts to life
still wander beyond the circle.

Now ceremony, now a game: *kai kai*
hands a pattern of crossed string
from one set of fingers to another,
a three-dimensional language
unnoticed by early explorers,
better grasped by those
who neither hear nor speak.

What challenged European ears remained
outside the mirror, flew in the face
of that which God-fearing men
believed could be.
What resisted imagination
remained impossible, unthinkable,
unknown.

Spoken language without a word for virgin,
absence of shame on a woman's shoulders,
colors of rock, grass, wind
erasing the hard rules
imposed by Church and State
when they tried to silence birds
or cancel a table set for three.

11

At the height of community, 20,000
may have lived and labored
on your accidental land.
Three hundred years carving and hauling
images that held a culture together,
makers and movers
trading art for extra food.

Statues others call similar
I see unique in every gesture:
height, girth, tilt of chin,
presence or depth of eyes,
angle of nose, expression on lips.
Beings as different from one another
as the ancestors they honor.

So who threw the massive figures down
and why?
Again the stories rise and fall,
memory and science
gnawing at lichen-covered rock.
Clan against clan? Artisans rebelling
against those who commissioned their work?

12

At Orongo the winds blow fierce enough
to sweep me from *Rano Kau's* lip
to the black rocks spitting spray
1,000 feet below. Along the narrow
strip of land between crater and sea

grass covers the Birdman houses
waiting in bermed repose.

Motu Kao Kao's guano-spattered pinnacle
rises from foam-tipped waves
and a fishing boat with five or six men
is a toy as it rocks and bobs
off its starboard side.
Power and defeat still echo
from these heights to the scene of the crime.

Makemake holds court on rock face weathered
by years, wind, rain and a chant
still heard in hearts that call
across pulled overlay of time. *Manu tara,*
sooty tern still return to their rookery
on *Motu Nui* where brave ghosts
swim back with eggs held high.

Female children, their legs spread wide,
still pose for the priests
who imprint their sex on stone.
Komari—the vulva glyphs—still
send their *mana* across a land
where men rule
and women birth children year by year.

13

The massive statues dead, this new ritual
gained in fervor, proclaiming
Tangata Manu winner from a winning clan
who lived in well-served isolation
until another spring unfolded and another youth

retrieved a new brown-spotted egg,
gaining prestige for the following year.

Revelers, dancers and chanters supported
the warriors and their servants.
The warriors gained or lost but their servants
like the carvers before them
braved the shark-infested waters,
sheltered in island caves,
swam back, the winning egg in hand.

Finally the Birdman cult also bowed
to depletion of time
and all the old ways faded
beneath the weight of unrecorded history.
If the Chilean supply ship fails to dock
flour is scarce. When planes land
the islanders gather to see who's come.

14

Was it village or class war finally put an end
to Rapa Nui's golden years,
hunger, despair, external rage
or intimate despair?
The statues cast face down
no longer confront descendants,
mana streaming from their eroding eyes.

The great figures, splayed at the foot
of their crumbling *ahu*
relax in volcanic soil,
earth fills sockets

where eyes once shot their power
straight to waiting hearts.
Wind cries.

The sea stretches to a circular horizon
from Rapa Nui's pink sand coves
and craggy cliffs
undoing themselves to foam.
Sea of a blue that has no name,
a dozen blues, no name for any.
Beyond cobalt. Beyond turquoise.

Gift for a new era, when the essence
of giving shifts.
No longer will we draw
heat and breath
from lovers or progeny,
but fill ourselves with the time of the *moai*
walking home.

15

Today, dogs that belong to everyone
and no one, sleek-coated dogs
roam the streets of *Hanga Roa*.
Rider-less horses gallop dusty sidewalks,
wait at unmarked crossings,
and look both ways before moving on.
Cattle graze among the fallen *moai*.

The tiny airport at *Hanga Roa* boasts
long Pacific runway:
alternative touch down

for the U.S. space shuttle if weather denies it
Cape Canaveral or California's coast.
Commercial flights to Tahiti and Chile
negotiate each new day.

As our plane descends, nosing toward tarmac
on your tiny triangle of land,
or lifts into the Pacific sky
headed for places in touch with other places,
a thick veil of time closes behind me,
eyes and ears shift and I breathe again:
that familiar register.

16

Now my dreams become places or a place
where time slips between grasses
choking the doors to secret harbors
of image, language, memory.
Barriers dissolve. A great shudder
invites me in, then throws
my body against itself.

What I saw, heard, felt, imprints itself
on the underside of skin.
What I left behind stays with me
in unexpected gravure.
By some arbitrary trick
I gained then lost four hours
for Rapa Nui's clocks strike Albuquerque time.

Rapa Nui's silent *moai* reach
from mysterious birth and death

across the waters of a cold Pacific
to where I wait
un-resigned to fading memory,
awkward, trembling, moved
to permanent response.

Storyline

1

Chaos below the Third Avenue El
fixes a harness across her breast.
Mother can't risk her breaking loose,
sudden screech of traffic or some strange hand,
doesn't know grandfather already enters
her invisible rooms.
Later she tears the straps,
defines direction as anywhere bad girls go.

She comes by stubbornness honestly,
remembers all her mother needed to hear
was: Don't visit Bolivia
there's been a revolution,
and family-strong
they cross the *altiplano* on a winter train,
descending to *La Paz*,
one corpse still swinging from a metal post.

Surely she imagines that corpse
woven deftly into her storyline,
images serving her writer's eye
as scenes multiply:
sleeping naked on sun-baked desert rock,
exploring ghost towns,
and the tongues of boys
no older and much less brave than she.

2

Time to move stage left, she travels
to a distant city
where artists work in cold-water lofts
meaning lifts itself in paint
and early poems
breathe pussy-willow shy.
She listens, lays down, stands up
and gives birth to a son
who forever after makes her two.

Her storyline curves outward, left again
and south to a different sound
whose syllables refuse
to come in from the rain
and inhabit her poems
but teach her to know and love
in another voice, stand with
those bludgeoned by the monster
she sees each time she opens her eyes.

Tlaloc lashed to an eighteen-wheeler
circles the place
Quetzalcoatl plays with serpent and *nopal,*
water pours from blue sky.
The poet who's lost his voice
tells her this and she is there,
living the scene he utters:
poor tongue longing for easier speech.

Pentimento walls catch white doves
in flight,
target splashes of red paint,

a *plaza* where hundreds die,
milk pail at dawn and death
falling either side of an ominous fence.
Later that fence moves north
splits a nation: language
unfit for any poem.

3

Then an island draws her to righteousness,
storylines compete
and children *nacen para ser felices*,
born to be happy in the words of revolution.
Map cut from the fabric of world,
energy flowing in every direction
sugar today
oil tomorrow,
fairness speaking her name.

She stuffs her script deep in pockets then
and deep in her children's pockets,
for now she is five
or six if she counts the man
but the man keeps changing,
ripping patches of her skin
as he disappears.
He cannot erase the woman
for she fashions a safe house,
only sometimes misplacing the key.

Sometimes she works so hard
to remember where she hides that key,
where flesh clings to spit and bone
and a small boat docks.

She and her children climb aboard
row with or against the current.
They follow her
until they don't anymore,
auditioning on their own.

4

Her story merges with
all the others then,
clamors like those in the poem
where one comes and begs the corpse:
Please don't die, get up and move,
and two come and ten and
a hundred thousand beseech the corpse,
and the dead man slowly rises to his feet
to inhabit another body,
battle or time.

Her storyline splits apart. She crosses borders
but pieces get left behind,
sprout small fingers and toes,
kick clods of earth,
find comfort in loneliness.
Men design master plans
and women make theirs
but the men swallow
the women's plans:
all in a good day's work.

She knows that un-chewed food
is wrong, sickens and pollutes.
Others begin to notice.

Courage replaces patience
on the list of good-girl traits,
and storylines come together
like magnets
connecting and growing
into a play with many characters,
all stitching promise to need.

We practice long and hard
from the turkey feathers
tied in ancient alcoves,
grain we mill
with our own hands
horizons calling us
through long canyons
into sunlit valleys
where we discover
a growing season.

5

Her storyline lingers among
nacatamales and dream,
tears that stopped flowing
come now in a cellular rush.
Trust clings to skin
stretched much too tight
and she gathers herself
as the B-movie man
becomes Commander in Chief,
promising an end to history.

She hauls her story north once more
to the place her umbilical cord

would welcome her
had her family kept tradition.
Even assimilated Jews depend on ritual
when weather mourns:
a lifeline for the lean times
come to a screeching halt
when all seems lost.

Strands of her story flung like loops
of rope: fishing nets on a Naxos pier
little red floaters
dotting the egg-yoke fiber
kept safe from Aegean blue.
One strand decides to fight
breathes hard against official dictum
declares herself home,
intends to stay.

Another reinvents love, retrieves trust
from a pile of worn garments
laid out by the fire
its flames rage high,
threaten to engulf her
if she chooses convention,
crooked speech closing her throat.

One strand whispers it's time to remember
time to focus
on the story without a name,
the one he told her never to tell
even when she was too young
too tender for words,
intuition alone
running interference in her veins.

6

Strands merge. Love comes.
Battles are won in quiet
as in pain.
Her story settles into place
where horror claims
the right to murder and hate.
Unspeakable acts
committed in her name.
But she says no.

All she can do is say no.
It is never enough.
While her storyline etches itself
in solid rock
her children weave their lives
and their children too,
and she loves the woman beside her
who loves her back.
Years hold them all.

Her storyline merges with those still walking
through jungles or to the edges of cliffs
follow ancient roads
carry babies up *moqui* steps
carved into vertical space.
She runs her tongue over teeth
ground low by sandstone in the corn
and wonders what language
will open her mouth.

She wants to believe every age
imposes death upon peoples
grabs more than its share

turns its back on water and on sun.
She wants to believe
we will survive, revive,
her great grandchildren free
to claim their places on another stage.

Feet Still Run

—Tlatelolco, October 2, 1968

1

Se les pasó la mano I heard someone say,
they went too far: irony as release
as if anyone believed
they'd fired to disperse the crowd.

It was early. We didn't know
the number of victims,
didn't know we would never know
who died that day.

White arm bands moving through the crowd,
bullets shattering air
over Aztec stone, between colonial walls
and modern apartment blocks.

Feet still run in every direction
leaving shoes, a beret, a handbag
trampled in the *Plaza de las tres culturas*
as the trapped still fight their way

into buildings, pound on doors, plead
with terrified neighbors
locked down against sudden war,
cutting lights, swallowing fear,

retreating to silence, pretending
the stairwells aren't sticky with blood

bodies aren't piled on bodies
two stories high.

2

What power does when threatened
is what we learned
that afternoon
thirty-nine years ago,

and displacement: rekindled images
of World War Two refugees
ghosts in slow lines
carrying households on their heads.

Parents making the rounds
of hospitals and morgues
staring into each bloated face
for signs of a son, a daughter.

Your knock at my door, your
random rush of words:
how you managed to take refuge
in one of the apartments

got out the next morning
hugging the arm
of the woman of the house
going for breakfast milk.

The 1968 Olympic Games
took place as promised.
White doves stenciled over graffiti
bleached the city for visiting crowds.

We entered night streets then
threw small bags of red paint
at each dove's breast.
And still, the city was mute.

3

Against the silence, whispers
of three hundred or a thousand dead,
students lined up behind the church
shot without charge or trial.

The Games went on, the athletes
only concerned
with winning their sport,
doing their country proud.
When two from the United States
raised their black-gloved fists
they where protesting
apartheid in South Africa

but we could pretend
they saw Mexico
stood with us
in our pain.

All these years later whispers, names,
numbers still crouch in alleys
wail across the *pedregal*
up the steep sides of mountain shantytowns

safely hidden
from a cosmopolitan city center

relentlessly competing its way
into the twenty-first century.

4

Every October second I wake remembering
what I cannot forget
have never forgotten
but store with all those other memories

pushed down where their sad mix
raises bile.
What power is capable of
when threatened

or in the words
of the *Tarahumara* man
who ran a thousand kilometers south
to lend his community's support:

"We've always known what they've done to us
but when they murder
their own sons and daughters
we know they are evil."

Neither our most devastating war
nor closest in time,
just me learning
how far they are willing to go.

How far they will go.

What I Tell the Young When They Ask

Resist
fictitious argument
luring or barking at your door
Don't ask your doctor
if seduction is right for you
only his wallet knows for sure.

Resist
turning away
from that which gleams in the sun
covers itself with unfamiliar cloth
or pronounces words
you do not understand.

Resist
don't ask don't tell
because it requires a dance of deception
steps on your toes
grinds them into a bed
of broken glass.

Resist
smoke and fire
water coveted in plastic bottles
a planet
too warm for life
too bleak for skin.

Resist
de-sexed corn, ancient grain
forced beneath the knife
regeneration taken by force

a trail of paper bullets
murdering surely as those of steel.

Resist
those who make
better bullets and bombs
clusters of pain
designed to kill
when hunger takes too long.

Resist
uniform or priestly collar
disguised on a scale of one to ten
books and tablets telling you
what will save you
from yourself.

Resist
my country right or wrong
men promising sound bites
answering only what they want you to know
then riding their rigged smiles
into a house of purest white.

Resist
the one on top
pitting his god his catchy phrase
a tune that taunts your face
spits in your eye
erasing the life-giving stories.

Resist
losing the ones
who know your name
call you from sleep

filling your mouth with music
when you wake.

Resist
rules created for you alone
and all your sisters and brothers
born and unborn
for they threaten
morning's fragile light.

Resist
disappearing into little boxes
of perfect safety
where risk is nowhere
greed is the prize
success thickens in your veins.

Resist
erasure of all our histories
for the sake of your
one and only life.
Listen to the small sounds.
Open your eyes.

FROM

My Town

(San Antonio: Wings Press, 2010)

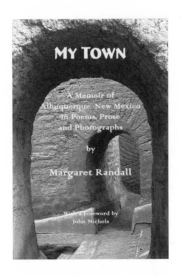

Nothing Was What It Pretended

Words I'd never heard took up residence
in my mouth.
Montaño, even if city signage
refused to put the tilda over the n,

names like *De Vargas, Cabeza de Vaca*
or *Juan Tabó*,
shepherds and assassins enshrined on street corners
unquestioned and mispronounced.

Indian words like *Acoma, Navajo*—now *Diné*—
or place names like *Canyon de Chelly*
the conquerors left us with
when they couldn't speak what they couldn't hear.

Names imposed: *Oñate, Coronado, Santa Fe.*
Another's holy faith bringing death
and leaving division, delighting
those who arrive on private planes.

Common words like *tijeras* and *frijoles*,
scissors and beans
began to quiver on my tongue,
stood easily in later years.

I too came from somewhere else,
a childhood far away,
with other sounds in my ears,
other familiars in my mouth.

The new words tested teeth, stretched lips
and exercised my landscape
until language caught meaning in its net
and I knew nothing was what it pretended.

This Could Have Happened

When the dog of invasion
bit my shoulder
I hardly felt his teeth.

It's his wild lunge and growl
still embedded in that tissue
of memory

behind my eyes,
the animal sound
of canines ripping flesh.

This could have happened
at the corner of 4th and Central
or where desert gathers

its sandy folds
against the mountain's face.
The place no longer holds

its coordinates
and so I wake each night
from a fever of battered dream.

Startling these Skies in 1054

More than fifteen thousand figures etched
by the ancients in this broad canyon
cover dark volcanic rock
at city's edge:
horned masks,

mountain lion trailing a snake behind one ear
and birds: one whose beak
extends to circle its floating perch
where message still rides the energy of time
and image bores through memory.

No tree or any other shade, only the ragged
rises and dips along a powdery path
hugging the shattered hillside,
our route surprised by a yellow cactus bloom
or desert lizard panting through the sage.

Volcanic boulders tumble this western escarpment
chipped to rust red beneath a polished surface,
line of craters above
and down below the grasses
growing through old lava.

You dub one image Big Head, what you also call
yourself: large square face, forehead
bearing one vertical worry line,
ears and legs and stand-up hair
protruding straight from bodiless stance.

Here a tight spiral may depict the supernova
startling these skies in 1054,

signify gathering place or starting point.
Shamanic figures
may or may not be shamans.

We have no record of how the people dressed,
what language they spoke,
whether theirs was art or signage,
a gallery left by men and women at work
or children at play.

My Albuquerque childhood knew nothing
of these petroglyphs,
this map destined for their time or ours.
Now law protects the pictures,
requires visitors respect their voice.

But today also brings the encroachment
of development, each new threat
a road will cut this canyon,
giving us yet another grid
of look-alike homes.

The mountain lion and bird, the snake
slithering across its baked surface
bear silent witness, resist.
They speak
and we are well advised to listen.

An Attitude I Never Learned

—for M.H.

Pure energy exploded the pom-poms she waved
across our high school football field.
It disappeared in a blaze of color, exuberant
leaps and an attitude I never learned.

All I wanted was to be like her, beyond popular:
cheerleader, homecoming attendant,
narrow waist
and eager bounce to her walk.

Her year's queen said goodbye in her wedding dress
from the depths of an early coffin.
Mine also died young
widowing the man she'd loved since thirteen.

Not a block from where we lived my idol's house
hid its perfect secrets,
only a year older
but light years beyond my fingertips.

Decades later, in generational meltdown
her only daughter became a friend,
time a collapsible telescope,
each of us awed by the story's missing half.

Slowly you revealed your childhood's underside:
mother cheerleader's anorexia and prescription pills,
drink and divorce
splitting your life in two.

When you told her of our friendship
she didn't remember me,
but before your mother died
you brought her to one of my readings

and in the restroom, at intermission, told her
I'd written eighty books.
"Well, how thick are they?"
Her question still echoes against the tiles.

Elaine

In my early years here in New Mexico, the person who most radically redirected my life was a visitor. More than any native, she taught me where I was and where I could go. All I needed was courage. Simply knowing her provided an abundance of that. Elaine de Kooning took one look at our watermelon mountains, cottonwood trees and old adobe houses and made herself at home. She took one look at me and brought me under her wing.

Elaine was a brilliant artist and sensually expansive woman, unashamed of those desires I'd been taught to hide between folds of unease and deception. Dance had made her fulsome body graceful and lithe, her muscled arms always reaching toward the work in progress. In the 1950s young girls were taught never to admit what we longed for. Boys were supposed to make the first move, and trouble stuck like river slime to the girls who succumbed or let them "go all the way." Although my aunt and her life companion lived together in Santa Fe, the word lesbian remained unspoken.

My own mother nurtured a succession of extra-marital affairs in awkward frenzy, semi-silence shrouding her frequent indiscretions. Elaine was the first woman I met who spoke openly and with disarming candor about desire; when several years after we met I headed for New York, she offered a long list of friends but warned me away from the occasional lover with whom she shared a special bond.

But intelligence and sex weren't the only or even most important arenas in which Elaine's outgoing nature redrew my interior map. Her identity in art, and attitude toward its process and practice, realigned my creative energies. As a visiting professor at our university's art department, her studio classes were always full. We met when I modeled for one of them, and she urged me to try my own hand at rendering the human figure. Elaine believed in freedom. Freedom of gesture, risk in everything she touched. She showed me that abandon long practiced becomes skill. I remember great rolls of butcher paper. She would tear off a large swatch and tell me to keep my eye on what I was drawing, be bold in my stroke, aim for attitude rather than detailed representation.

There were lessons about materials as well: only the best brushes and most expensive paints would do. Especially for beginners, Elaine always said. Good materials were particularly important for those who couldn't yet harness talent. Unless you knew what that lush exuberance felt like in your hand, how could you know what making art could be? Elaine's generosity led to her providing the best for many young artists: an expertly-stretched canvass or $50 brush. You were hooked by the time you understood that discipline was as necessary as pigment.

Like many from New York City, when she came to New Mexico Elaine couldn't drive. She bought a second-hand car and I and several others took turns teaching her to maneuver its idiosyncrasies. Drunk one night, she drove into her own living room. Passing her driving test was a problem. On her third try the traffic inspector was Irish. She beguilingly convinced him a third failure would discredit their shared national origin and obtained her license.

Later, in New York, throughout the years of our friendship I often dropped in on Elaine at her loft: sweatshop illegally turned living quarters and painting space combined. She continued painting while we talked, gossiped, laughed, conspired. Even as she stepped back from a work in progress, contemplating a problem area with the great power of intuition and analysis she honed throughout her life, her attention to our conversation was deeper and more to the point than what I got from anyone else. She went straight for the throat.

Elaine loved life. When I gave birth to Gregory she showered him with adoration and me with a year's worth of diaper service and anything else she could think of that would ease a single mother's life. Through Elaine my son became the mascot of the New York art world, attending gallery and museum openings in his white wicker basket. She thought his every move amazing.

Life for Elaine was just as valuable at the other end. When Caryl Chessman was condemned to die in California, Elaine threw herself into the campaign to save him. When he was executed she took to bed for a week. At every point along life's way, Elaine found reason to encourage and support all those who needed an injection of confidence, or save someone in danger of falling into the abyss. When my son was small and I needed the occasional babysitter, she explained how important hiring a recovering addict would be for the man's self-esteem. What more precious to entrust him with, she asked, than a beautiful baby? When a couple we knew couldn't take care of their little girl, Elaine found a childless couple in Texas to adopt her. If it favored human well-being, she could and would make anything happen.

Elaine never mentioned her father, except when she told the story of her mother leaving him. Marie was the traditional Irish Catholic and faithful mother of four until her children could make it on their own, but Elaine said she'd always been very clear she would take off one day. She'd even announced the future date, which no one took seriously. When that day came, she packed her bags and left. Once she no longer had to care for family, studying math and languages consumed the years she had left. Elaine said she was brilliant, and loved telling stories about the woman who had birthed her and was so ahead of her time. To her a woman going after what she needed and wanted was always to be celebrated.

Marie was proud of Elaine's accomplishments, although abstract expressionism was beyond her. I remember the day she found a larger than life-sized photo of Chessman's face among her daughter's things; it was mounted on canvass and had been used in a march against capital punishment. Marie said she was thrilled Elaine had returned to realistic portraiture.

This was long before the second wave of feminism swept many of us into its fervor. Like most of her female peers, Elaine didn't care to be called a woman artist. She was an artist, no more no less, and good as any man. The language of feminism wasn't something she ever adopted, yet whenever we talked about how women had to struggle for our rights, she was the first to admit the unfairness of society's gender assignments.

Elaine's sister Marjorie was her best friend and only true confidante, as well as the mother of the three nephews she showered with her own maternal exuberance. Her brothers Conrad and Peter were ready in the wings, part of that Irish family support that always seemed to bolster her. They too had children—I remember Peter's daughter Maude, a name that nestled in my consciousness—but Marjorie's Luke, Jon Pierre, and Mike were the clear inheritors of Elaine's largesse, and beneficiaries of her bountiful example.

In New Mexico my friendship with Elaine ushered me into a larger world, a dimension I've inhabited since. It was a world in which the most generous ideas were nurtured and what was off-limits for many seemed matter of fact. This included political concepts out of favor at the time. Art was valued, honesty was a virtue and anything was possible. If you came to Elaine with a problem, before you finished telling her about it she was actively involved in its solution. If you wondered whether to go this way or that, Elaine laughed and asked why choose?

In her early twenties, Elaine decided Willem de Kooning was the greatest painter of her generation. It was only logical they should fall in love and marry. She went with him to the experimental college at Black Mountain, North Carolina, and together they returned to New York City and a life of mid twentieth century cutting-edge creativity.

There was no question in Elaine's mind that Bill was the best. Long after they no longer lived together—he involved with a succession of other women and she with her own lover of the moment—she devoted her considerable talents to promoting his career. Elaine thought and wrote about art as brilliantly as she made it.

In her forties, her stint in New Mexico established a connection that remained vital as long as she lived. Her presence, friendship and encouragement touched and changed many local artists, sending us on paths we might not have had the courage to explore had she not made us believe they were our natural next steps. The vast blue sky and desert palette, for her, were canvasses upon which the surprising and magical happened.

Here ancient cultures and contemporary indigenous communities welcomed her home. At the Zuni Shalako one year we spent the night with the pueblo's governor and his family. He was an admirer of Willem de Kooning's work. His mother—I think Lewis was her last name—had been the first woman from Zuni to earn a college degree. Elaine and I spent that night in sleeping bags under the broad portal of the governor's home, rising at dawn to watch the dancers coming across the plain from a distant mountain retreat. Later she got Bill to send the governor a small painting in gratitude.

I had already dispensed with a first sad marriage during which my young husband and I had lived for a while in Spain. That's where I fell in love with bullfighting, influenced by Hemingway's romantic novels and my own early attraction to pageantry. Back in New Mexico I drove regularly to Ciudad Juárez, the Mexican border city six hours south, to attend Sunday fights at its *Plaza Monumental*. For a while I even wrote fight reviews for a California magazine dedicated to the brutal rite.

Elaine and I spent many weekends together in Juárez. We always stayed at the same hotel, drank tequila at the same bar, and gloried in the Sunday afternoon display with its bravado and theater. Young and unperturbed by such cruelty to animals, I still subscribed to the excitement of the dubious drama with its predetermined outcome. Elaine would spend the entire afternoon sketching the dramatic movements of bejeweled fighter and angry animal. Those sketches led to one of her best-known series of paintings; and they in turn to her fascination with much more ancient bulls. Creative chutzpah gained her entrance to the caves at Lascaux long after they were closed to the public.

Elaine also loved painting athletes—loved the male body in action—and in New York we often went to Madison Square Garden to watch basketball or track. I remember going with her to see U.S. American John Thomas and Soviet Valery Brumel compete with one another. It was Brumel's birthday and he jumped seven feet six inches, extraordinary for the early 1960s. Later she did a portrait of President John F. Kennedy, spending many hours sketching him as he went about the affairs of state. When I lived in Cuba she asked if I thought I could wangle her a chance to paint Fidel. I tried but didn't succeed.

Years passed. I lived in Mexico, Cuba and Nicaragua before returning to New Mexico in 1984. Elaine continued to paint and show, earning a place for herself among the male artists—albeit inevitably a secondary place. One of Bill de Kooning's lovers gave birth to the child Elaine always dreamed of but never had. She and he continued to live separately, although joined by an unbreakable bond; toward the end of his life she moved back in, got him to stop drinking as she had years before, and jealously oversaw his care. By then dementia had taken much of Bill's mind, yet he continued to paint every day. She didn't need language to predict his needs. Then, surprisingly, she died before he did, consumed by the cigarettes she never could give up.

When the U.S. government tried to deport me because of ideas expressed in a number of my books, Elaine took a portrait of me she had done in 1960 and reproduced it as a high-quality poster to be sold to benefit my struggle. She hadn't dated the image back when she painted it, and just before sending it to the printer added her signature "E de K" and "1963" at the bottom. I knew she'd painted it in 1960; I was pregnant with Gregory at the time. I told Elaine I was sure of the earlier date but she stubbornly stuck to 1963.

The last time Elaine and I saw one another she must already have been ill, but hid it well. I visited her at the beautiful East Hampton home and studio where she lived in later years. I'd brought some of my photographs and we made a trade. By this time I was living with a woman. I introduced my partner, and Elaine looked me straight in the eye and assured me she knew exactly why two women might choose to be together: there weren't that many good men anymore, she said. For the first and only time in our long friendship I made a conscious decision not to dispute the observation. There was too much else to talk about.

Ever Ready to Fly

In years to come I'd learn the world could change,
follow a route of broken bodies
and searing hope,
seek those ridges of place and time
where travelers swallow fear
to carve impossible trails
through jungles of pain.

Growing up I knew nothing of red paint
aimed at the breasts of white doves
stenciled on Mexico's bullet-riddled walls,
nothing of kids not much older than me
dying for the crime of youth on Managua's streets,
throwing their only bodies
at generations of shame.

In 1953 I attended my city's whitest school,
dreamed of being homecoming queen,
wrote romantic poems
with church bells and tumbleweed
while Cubans I would embrace one day
made their first assault upon a dictator
who gave new meaning to an eye for an eye.

Words spoken only by desert rock back then,
words I neither heard nor understood,
wove a fabric keeping me warm in winter
and free of summer fevers
until I caught up with myself,
took risk in hand
and went in search of air.

Albuquerque accompanied me like a small tattoo,
bird or flower on my left shoulder,
this childhood city
where circumstance of birth
prepared me for nothing
but freed a spirit
ever ready to fly.

Margaret in 2010.
St. Mark's Poetry Project, New York City.

FROM

Something's Wrong with the Cornfields

(Great Britain: Skylight Press, 2011)

Your Frightened Eyes

A great fish swims across the sky
its dark outline
hinting at fanciful design
of Chinese New Year splendor,
giant tail propelling it side to side
as it slithers past the tops
of tall buildings.

Pink-tinged early morning clouds
snag the curve of one fin,
scales like embossed flowers
dance on its enormous body.
As it disappears beyond the tree line
a blazing ball of sun
lifts itself from the horizon.

I touch your elbow, grab your arm,
try to say the word fish
with lips that utter no sound.
You don't look to the sky
but keep your frightened eyes on mine,
the question in them
heavy with fearful answer.

Something's Wrong with the Cornfields

Something's wrong with the cornfields.
In Utah's wide valleys
between red rock walls
wind works
to stir a brush-cut of tassels.
Nothing moves.

Defiant, their strange offering
recalls molded plastic,
each spear exact height
of the next.
Dense thicket of green plants,
identical.

Winds unable to bend a stalk
carry altered seed and pollen.
Chemicals vanquish borer larvae,
inhabit milk of corn-fed cows,
poison those who drink,
erase the butterflies.

We witness the terror
of genetic engineering
seeds ripped from history
splitting threads of continuity.
Earth Mother's hands
tied behind her back.

Memories of the family *milpa*,
childhood images of Kansas,
India's suiciding farmers.

A threat to generations
teaching us to fear
designer sustenance.

I dream a stash of ancient cobs
chewed clean by teeth
and grit of sand
eight hundred years ago.
Escalante's shallow stone basin
calls me home.

Whoever We Are

Purple shadows gather splayed boulders
into generous fists.
Sun burns a surface of rabbit brush and sage,
throwing kaleidoscope of green
at glistening sand.

Mist rises off water against still-blossoming sky
where dark silhouettes of cranes unbend
their backward knees,
long beaks pecking seed.
Distant mountains simmering.

Fitted between the walls of houses,
squeezed into furniture
built for other bodies,
shuttled through streets
that never change their minds,
we long for simple.

A day that begins at dawn and ends
when the last stripe of gold
disappears from the lip of canyon wall.
Rock impregnated with heat,
welcoming touch.

But consider the wildebeest's calculation,
calf clasped in belly waiting for the rains,
or its newborn
expected to run and keep up
fifteen minutes after birth.
Consider the last whooping crane
searching for its mate.

Whoever we are.
Whatever we do.

Warp and Weft

for Joy Harjo

You are right. They are wrong.
You prepare yourself well,
take your place
with evidence of pure heart,
witnesses who saw clearly
and are willing to speak
on your behalf.

But smug and twisted power
hides behind its blind of lies
disguised as a blanket
whose warp and weft collide,
its colors wrong.
Tradition can be a loaded gun.

Some call it Boys Will Be Boys,
others Might Makes Right,
Policing the World,
Academia, or simply The System.
You are supposed to be afraid.
They play by rules
they change at will.

In homespun wool and human hair,
colors from rock and living plant
earth and sky—ignored by them—
take you in their arms,
pull you to full height,
soothe muscle, tendon, heart.

They may win the battle
but not the war
because we do not acknowledge
their war
and their win is a fleck of lint
you brush from one brave sleeve.

Remaining on My Skin

Between faint dent in my cheek
and this Northern Sonora desert
a Red Tail hawk
climbs into sky
and boulders turn purple
as they journey down.

We came together to this place.
No one knows my stutter of words
better than you.
No one else
can finish my trailing sentence
before I turn it out to pasture.

I am afraid my shadow
will eat itself
before dawn opens again,
the concentric lines
of a Geological Survey map
remaining on my skin.

Take me here when it is finished,
love,
not like the writer who wanted
coyotes and carrion birds at his bones
but sweetly: every season shining in our eyes.

Memory Itself

The word cedar creeps from itchy wiggly toes
through thighs, belly,
moves into diaphragm
and quivers along the hanging undersides
of aging arms.

It begins a rich reddish brown—no surprise—
but quickly sends off yellow sparks
turning to slow gold
before it withers and dies
in a patchwork of green and black.

Here I stop to slow my breath: oxidization
turns pale rock to orange,
the cactus flower's silky pink,
and white clouds reflect
in the pool of water at my feet.

The word wellbeing screeches to a halt
inches from my face.
Sandbar never was cream or tan
but a quilt of leaping question marks,
exhausted when heat strays.

I wash my hands again and again,
their worn skin barely resists
such affront to tired cells.
Yet nothing can change
their sad color:

helpless, enraged, astonished
by the calculated crimes
of those who pretend to lead
while destroying the nest
every one of us must share.

Memory loses its shape, I imagine
a colorless world
empty of pigment, no palette at all,
translucent absence
forward and backward in time.

Long Goodbye to the Paper Page

I will not write another poem
I say almost weekly
with varying degrees
of certainty.

Not me, not another book,
nothing at all
that will be read
by others,

such anticipation
held in hand
by those looking
for answer or escape.

Special smell and feel of books,
the weight of their pages
and resistance to fingers
that turn them

slowly, thoughtfully,
seeking knowledge
or feeling,
exotic or familiar accent,

perhaps accompaniment
to a cup of tea
or quiet time
before a fire.

Electronic media is
our reading future,
Kindle highlights
take the curious

everywhere,
draw the rainbow
across a vast sky.
But where will memory hide,

where retrieve that moment
we may sit and gaze
at letters on paper,
their ordinary shapes?
Why does this poem end
with precisely this word,
that sigh
or broken twig?

No more books.
No more poems.
A claim that bears
repeating.

Small Rituals

In predawn quiet I gather
and draw about me
this collection of small rituals:
worn sheepskin slippers,
glasses accessible
because I know
exactly where I placed them
on the bench beside my bed.

Other less-welcome items
come along for the ride:
a small scab
pulling taut
the skin on my neck
where biopsy brought good news
but aging flesh
retards the healing process.

Cracking finger joints
warm to brave service
and upright posture
makes its own demands
as I flick dried sleep
from my eyes
and swallow the sticky film
that coats my tongue.

It is three a.m.
I head for my studio
where the touch
of a single key

brings computer screen to life
and welcomes me
to yet another chance
to get it right.

Here the larger rituals
talk too loud
and much too fast.
I unfold memory,
encourage its cooperation
and balance it
on sturdy knees
where it cannot get away.

Memory looks up at me
and laughs
then yawns.
Today's puzzle requires
the same input code
as yesterday.
Then I know I will have
another opportunity

to finish the Great American Poem
or tell myself
it's okay:
tomorrow is another day
whose familiar small
and overwhelming rituals
will comfort
or get in my way.

Margaret in 2012.
At Beyond Baroque, Venice, California.

FROM

As If the Empty Chair
Poems for the disappeared
Como si la silla vacia
Poemas para los
desaparecidos

(San Antonio: Wings Press, 2011)

AS IF THE EMPTY CHAIR

Poems for the disappeared

COMO SI LA SILLA VACÍA

Poemas para los desaparecidos

Margaret Randall

Disappeared

A word without hands or feet,
nothing to run with,
no warm grip
for trembling fingers,
a lonely word,
blood rushing to its head,
lurching forward on raw stumps
before collapsing
in a heap of fading questions.

A word that has lost its thunder
like the felled tree
where no ear
registers its crash
to forest floor,
ritual quiet
where even the softness
of velvet
causes the skin to bruise.

A word unable to describe
its burden of loss,
asthma
when it tries to speak,
frozen in time
though flecked with a fire
that burns
the millions of hands
reaching to embrace its pain.

Thirty-two years ago Rodolfo
vanished out of his life
in Buenos Aires, one last *mate*
cupped in his palm,
one last sip
through the silver straw,
no more letters to public opinion,
not another step another breath
through our long winter of despair.

Now we read "Argentina won't extradite
'Dirty War' officer":
the headline's dubious punctuation
a stand-in for torn limbs,
words suspended in maybe
or twisted promise,
a blade so polished and sleek
it severs your head
with only a nod to your heart.

Conviction and prison likely now
for that Blond Angel of Death
and other criminals
this year's government finds
accountable for your fate
and that of 30,000 others,
writers or not, public figures
or simply sons and daughters,
lovers and workers

who still walk the scarred streets
of a city peopled by ghosts,
whispered conversation,

truncated songs
whose fading words
can only be read on old walls
or echo inside the heads
of those who remain:
still searching, still in love.

As If the Empty Chair

Can't we just put it behind us,
those untouched ask,
but where is behind,
in what cardinal direction
does it stand,
what weather endure,
which intersection
of latitude and longitude,
crosshairs coming together
upon its hungry face?

Can't we just move on,
as if the empty chair
isn't tucked beneath table rim,
that side of the bed isn't barren and cold
or the mirror reflecting a single face
doesn't taunt these lives
we inhabit:
uneasy occupants
paying in installments
for what we no longer own.

Without him, without her,
without those plucked
from this air we breathe
we no longer possess our lives
the space that surrounds us,
sweet sounds of street or field.
Without them
we cannot move on,
for where will they find us
when they stumble home?

Seasons

Autumn came crude that year,
its temperature cutting flesh.
Echoes remained,
humming in eardrums,
taunting the usefulness of hands.
Leaves escaped branches,
unable to resign themselves
to no return.

Winter was worse.
Feet tingled
beneath the heavy felt
draped over tables
with their poor offerings
of *mate* and biscuits,
while outside our bodies
froze in place.

Spring should have brought relief
but didn't.
Each tulip,
each crocus bud
reminded us
she's not here
to absorb their color,
embrace their eager hope.

Summer completed a void
we knew would be followed
by another,

less vivid perhaps
than the one before
but burying the same chill
beneath our skin,
the same loss.

Seasons fall apart.
They say you are not at home
until you have lived in a house
through all four seasons.
What they don't say is
you are never at home
when a part of that home
has been taken.

Someone Lives

If I can say I remember
someone lives.
Someone breathes
as my lungs contract
and expand.
Someone is at home in space,
holds out hands
palms up.

Palms down or dropped
to my side
erase a lifetime
of moments,
easy sequence
from birth to natural death,
flickering of energy
where all directions thrive.

If I can say I remember
I do remember,
and the suddenly-vanished
—decades ago or yesterday—
move into light once more.
It is the precious task
their dead fingers
imprint upon my own.

FROM

Ruins

(Albuquerque: University of New Mexico Press, 2011)

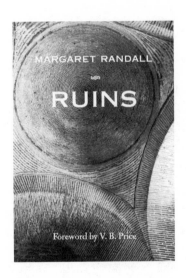

Places We Call Home

This is the center, the great hub, its spokes
moving along arrow-straight roads
to the cardinal directions.
Roads wide as runways, perhaps
more for ritual than travel,
to a thousand outlier communities
north as far as Betatakin and Kiet Seel,
south to Paquimé.

The Great Houses stand either side of this
broad wash, under hovering cliffs
and sky that is always blue,
even when roiling clouds
bulk before releasing
infrequent rain.
On the desert water can kill
as surely as it saves.

Pueblo Bonito, Chetro Ketl, Kin Kletso,
Pueblo Alto and Casa Rinconada:
names that inhabit the mouth
or slip off the tongue
from early inhabitants, explorers
and scholars, sometimes
reflecting what happened here
and sometimes not.

Shimmying up the long fracture of rock
above Pueblo Bonito my camera pack
catches in the narrow crack.
I turn to free myself and move

to where I can look down
on the half-moon like a scale model,
its tiny figures appearing
and disappearing room to room.

I have come here with the woman
I love, intending to camp
then dissuaded by mosquitoes.
With grandchildren I must convince
to leave broken pottery where it lies.
Friends who suffer in the midday heat
or cannot still
their racing hearts.

Each visit I look for the mountain lion:
tiny petroglyph figure on the cliff
that borders a trail
linking one house with another.
Each visit I run my hand
the length of Chetro Ketle's wall,
ponder its array of kivas or strain
to glimpse the moqui steps I'll never climb.

January 22, 1941: I was four years old
when 30,000 tons of rock
fractured and fell on Pueblo Bonito
destroying its north wall
and 65 rooms. What other
Chaco dates weave in and out
of mine, before during
or beyond my passage?

There will always be a next time,
I tell myself, another visit

to contemplate Wetherill's shame
or learn about the 18.6-year intervals
when earth and sky align
and a sliver of light
descends a wall,
changing the course of prehistory.

Here swallows nest in little pockets of mud
on sandstone walls that drip
with desert varnish,
petroglyphs bear sad bullet holes,
each season picks up where
the one before it vanished,
and the sun always keeps
its promise to itself.

Maybe I lived here once or visited
from north or south.
Maybe the tiny turquoise bead
you placed in my hand
is from a string I wore
eight hundred years ago.
Maybe we all return
to the places we call home.

Kiet Seel

for Mark Behr

Almost too late you say let's go,
you'll carry 60 or 70 pounds
to my 20, urge me to make
the reservation: between
May and September they allow
20 hikers a day.

I study maps, consider spring rains
and what I will prepare
for us to eat. Keep it light, I think,
my heart already racing
toward that place where one giant pine
kept people in or out.

Eighteen half-mile markers lead us
through shifting sand,
animal tracks and wildflowers
coax us on.
Kiet Seel stands as it has for centuries
in its alcove above the delta.

Strange to think of delta in this desert
but the river that threatens us
with quicksand
would have been bigger then,
feeding patches of corn and beans,
wetting the pinched lips of clay pots.

It is those pots, some of them broken
but placed where they might have been,
those pots and cobs cleaned of corn
that lure us where we imagine
a man lifting a beam, a woman grinding,
a child turning her face to ours.

On tough hikes there is always
that moment I must complain
I can't go on. Stop. Breathe.
Loosen the straps squeezing shoulders
and will. Then stand
and proceed without another word.

Always a second breath, fuller
than the first,
ready to carry me through
as I move ahead,
walking in front of you now,
lulled by the thud of heavy boots.

When we reach the stand of Gambel oak
and tiny campsite
we know it can't be far,
leave our packs,
stretch aching bodies
and ford one last creek crossing,

hurrying up to wait before the Hogan gate,
coughing in the Navajo way of saying
we are here, until a young man
emerges to take us through
a final spread of undergrowth
where the ruin waits.

And there she is, as 800 years ago
when men and women worked
and children played
on the broad avenue
that fronts the complex
of kivas, rooms and walls.

Who knew we would have to climb
a seventy-foot ladder, almost vertical
to enter our destination?
We exchange a look but drip cold sweat
and meet the challenge
without a word.

Precious hours walking from room
to room, tracing painted turkeys
with our eyes, imagining bright macaws
squawking from poles that rise
beside perfect windows, doors
barely tall enough to let a body through.

Time slows then stops as the Navajo caretaker
tells us why his grandfather
didn't want him to take this job,
disturb the spirits
who still reside
within these walls.

That night we watch from camp
as shadows fill the space
where Kiet Seel was or is,
warm ourselves
in the solar-powered pit toilet
before taking off at dawn.

The return hike is lighter and faster
as we recognize features of the land
and retrieve stashed water bottles,
the people of the delta
and their habitat
homesteading in our eyes.

Cursive Writing and Old Slide-Rules

One day I will walk in a graveyard
where cursive writing and old slide-rules
sleep beneath dead leaves
and rain-soaked earth.

Elaine's chortling laugh, one phrase
from a Brandenburg concerto
that once lifted my heart
above cacophony that sweeps

anonymous streets, shielding
our human register from touch.
I may stop to pay tribute
to crinolines and cashmere sweater sets,

egg beaters, rotary phones, transistor
radios and old typewriters
their red and black ribbons
floating spirals

over moss-covered stones on misty nights.
I may recall an IBM Selectric,
the raised letters of its tired steel ball
glistening in the light of a waning moon.

The permanently signaling left arm
thrusts from the window of a 1941 Ford,
its upholstery smelling faintly
of burnt plush.

A 78 rpm record spins beneath
the diamond tip of a tiny needle
recreating Patsy Cline's familiar sound
in my astonished ears.

Daughters of the American Revolution
refuse Constitution Hall
to Marian Anderson's perfect voice
and Eleanor Roosevelt

makes it right by inviting her to sing
before Lincoln's imposing figure
where 75,000—black and white—
receive her offended voice.

Weekly newsreels at the RKO, Superman
vanquishing Khrushchev, Walkmans
their ear plugs deafening an era,
The Joy of Cooking, 1ˢᵗ edition,

and casseroles topped with thick slices
of Velveeta cheese. Carnation corsages
dyed two-tone pink to match
a strapless prom gown lost to memory.

Where will I find one reason to nourish
the hope that tomorrow's graveyards
may imprison darker relics, dangerous
even in their after-life:

all those advertising claims, the lies
of those we love who love us back,
our hatred of children
and this grim currency of violence?

When will we bury greed, erase our fear
of women and difference, trust ourselves,
design a final resting place
for war?

Dare I hope noise camouflaged as ideas
dogma or commanding truth
will one day fail to greet me
as I rise each morning

and make my stumbling way through
digital possibility, hold tight
to the Mohawk two-wheeler,
faint oiled skin of that first Royal portable

or your green rayon dress, Mother,
with its white rope pattern
still so comforting to my young
and trusting cheek?

Thank You

Thank you for the perfect call
of the canyon wren
and her mate's perfect response.
For that line
where water caresses rock
rising and falling
the breadth of a canyon wall.
Thank you for explosion of birth
times four.
The portal where I disappear
into a painting by Arshile Gorky
even as I stand
on the outside looking in.
Thank you oh thank you
for my sleep
curled around your sleep
your skin's temperature,
Bach's clavichord
journeying from ear to heart
and back,
its sound entering every pore
drawing desire
into my throat.
Thank you for the grandchild's smile
so like his father's or mother's
but more alive.
For the day we finally win
what should have been ours
from birth
and the hope sustaining us
each time we lose.

The poem that pulls me
into the moment
instead of telling me about it.
Thank you for helping me know
there is no one to thank
but all of us
carrying memory on our shoulders
our dead moving beside us
whispering in our ears.

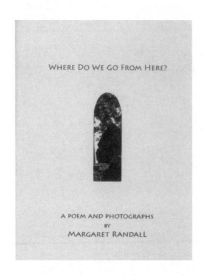

Where Do We Go From Here?
(San Antonio: Wings Press, 2012)
Miniature chapbook

Daughter of Lady Jaguar Shark
(San Antonio: Wings Press, 2013)
Miniature chapbook

FROM

The Rhizome as a Field of Broken Bones

(San Antonio: Wings Press, 2013)

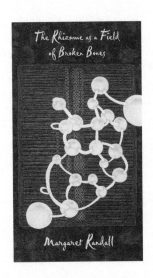

The Rhizome as a Field of Broken Bones

From hops to orchids,
ginger to the sanctified bloom
we call Lily of the Valley
a horizontal stem
or root mass
moves beneath the ground,
feeling its way,
choosing where it will wake and rise
in yet another multiplying mirror
we hold to history.

The ancient Greeks gave us
this anatomy: rhizome
as key to vegetable resistance.
Utah's Pando colony
of Quaking Aspen
a million years young.
Neither foragers, insects,
fungus nor fire
shatters the design
of its secret hiding place.

At this level of our fractal universe
elegant fern
and plebian Bermuda grass,
purple nut sedge
or obstinate poison oak
wait at trail edge
for the next hiker's
bare legs:
all speak the language of rhizome
to our grateful ears.

We who see a field
of broken bones
view pale faces
on memory's imprint
befriend the rhizome:
neither beginning nor end.
Balanced at midpoint,
it resists chronology
and we claim our place
as nomads on a savage map of risk.

Not linear narrative but radiant grid
where four dimensional images dance
and one rain forest butterfly
bloats a Kansas funnel cloud
with energy unmeasured
by the lab scientist
willing to consider
a million lives collateral damage,
intent only on his chance
at the big prize.

Imagine you are a child
in Phnom Penh,
the skulls creeping rootstalks,
one sprouting another
from its node
of ideology gone insane,
twenty sprouting a thousand,
two million, a landscape
where above ground and below
a single terror moves.

Pull your only legacy back
through Treblinka's classrooms

where desperate teachers
help children wrap memory
paint freedom
on comforting squares of paper.
Wander among piles of shoes,
mountains of human hair,
each new node
an evil birthing.

Rest yourself in phantom Elazig,
now Turkey in denial,
where thousands of Armenians
lived and loved
before the genocide.
Contemplate the sharp edge
of a Rwandan machete
and try to remember if you
wielded the weapon or knew its steel
against your throat.

Enter this complex community
through its back door,
breach its rockiest border
and break the hold
steep systems of convention
have on you.
Open yourself
to time
in every dimension.
Welcome a new home.

Today I am one more
body of water
filling available space,

trickling down
through fissure and gap
toward a new map,
eroding what stands in my way.
You may try to interrupt my dance
but your ugly language
leaves no signature.

Canary in the Mine 1

Chained to a School Board desk in Tucson, Arizona,
students protest the erasure of *In Lak Ech*—
You Are My Other Me.
Democracy beats them bloody.

Devious as Helen at Troy, Western Civ
and Last Supper pop-ups,
memory ancient as *maize*
and dangerous as who we know we are.

Following Nogales, Tucson, Chicago and north,
law becomes hate's trail of crumbs.
The walking dead climb aboard
an underground train of hope.

Dark ghosts breach borders rigged by men
on monumental steeds
who keep order
in the history we're taught.

Beyond the front-line border wall
invisible replicas fall like dominoes
across the next ridge and the next.
On the desert all the borders die.

Every brown child who fears questions,
papers, and the pale green *migra* van,
every child of every hue taught nothing
but how to score on the master's test,

marks time because thinking has turned
dangerous and living by the rules
foolproof prelude
to a future where none will hear the song.

When floodwaters recede and fire turns to ash,
when they come to see what's left
they will find a million dead canaries:
singing in perfect harmony.

Mother Triptych

1

Supermarket neon claimed our neurons,
loss keeping you close to me
until you stopped:
Ginsberg's vision of Whitman
Old White Beard
among the vegetables.

You weren't Whitman but my mother.
I looked back and watched you lift
one ugly Portobello
by its thick stem,
your knobby hand clenched
just below its spreading threat of flesh.

Turning it slowly to your gaze,
perhaps wondering
why I am so afraid, perhaps knowing.
One aisle distant then
I swallowed memory trying to believe
you wouldn't move my way.

You put the mushroom back
pretended I hadn't seen
and we continued buying food
while I kept battering you
with small hurts, questions unanswered
before or since your death.

2

You asked about the big new County Courthouse
bricks like sands of a desert we both love,
so many new buildings,
said you never noticed it before.

I told you we passed it every week,
maybe you don't remember,
strange pleasure of barbed words
only now echoing remorse.

Back then I wanted you to feel the shame
of memory loss
like images fallen beneath the waistband
of your old striped chambray skirt,

like your sad prosthetic breast
lodged there once on a walk
we took along Grand Canyon's rim,
Dad still with us, anguish in your eyes.

You didn't live to hear about the scandal,
the senator who made millions
off that courthouse job,
didn't live to hear he's serving time:

the kind of news festooning
your shorter days
as more new buildings cut the skyline
of this city you wouldn't recognize.

3

We bought our little bags of mild green *chile*
at Sitchler's seasonal stand
a block from your Assisted Living,

until a guy in a white truck tall on super tires
blocked right then left and shrieked a menacing laugh
refusing to let us leave.

You sat small and silent when I opened my door
climbed from the driver's seat
and walked to his window

heart thundering, face on fire
steadying my voice
as I told him you were 96.

You're scaring my mother I said,
not you're scaring me,
then walked slow as I could

back to our car where I waited
for him to back up
and when he didn't

restarted my engine, inched around
his testosterone display
never taking my eyes from the ugly grin

and not once glancing at you, Mother,
holding your breath in the seat to my right
three years empty now.

Not Quite Blood

Not quite blood
but more than salt,
top tooth
into lower lip

bite just short
of breaking skin.
This is my
thinking hard

gesture, my
give me time
to get this right
device,

aimed at anyone
tempted to interrupt
or standing in the way
of halting progress

and well this side
of *you're done*:
senility's semaphore:
no more words at all.

Our Customs

Recoil at humans eating humans, *cannibal*
a word that holds repulsion in its craw
even when speaking of a people
whose culture eludes us
through today's myopic prism.

Evidence of boiling human skulls in pots
unearthed at Ancestral Puebloan sites
brings science to philosophical assumption.
Judge not, lest you be judged
the wise man said, but they cannot judge

who are safely dead. Neither titillation
nor indignation grab my heart,
intent and circumstance germane
to what we believe and how we proceed
upon this grieving land.

I prefer to think about chocolate making
its addictive way from purple pods
on Andean lowland trees,
moving along Xochimilco's waterways,
from the stones of Tenochtitlán and Teotihuácan,

stopping to rest at Guachimontones and Paquimé,
carried in salivating bags, its aroma escaping
their loose weaves, grated into those same
clay pots, mixed with maize or spring water
deep in the alcove at Kiet Seel.

With a diet of corn and squash and beans,
occasional deer or rabbit and rare luxury
of nuts, the dark delight must have been
reserved for feasts that marked birth,
death, coming of age or victory in war.

Mexico's Cora people trace the origin of *chile*
to a long-ago banquet where a man,
brave in those acts where men excel,
wiped sweat from his genitals, brought fingers
to lips and tasted the world's first hot sauce.

I bring my fingers to eager lips, taste chocolate
two millennia before Black Forest Cake,
perfect éclair, Godiva, or Dairy Queen Soft-Serve,
when seed and pod and root still held the poetry
of breath and tongue in magical embrace.

Ten centuries beyond that residue of bone on clay
and chocolate's journey north,
we humans still devour one another
in ways I do not wish to honor in a poem
nor will I place our customs above theirs.

Colophon

Helvetica, Bodoni or Arial Black uncurl
in the colophon of this gem-like book.
How the poem inhabits the page,
its sounds and silences standing proud.

One last chance to make sure the reader
spends a moment contemplating form
as well as content, listens for
barely audible breath or hard U turn.

Form and content: two wings of a bird
who carries my heart in its sharp beak,
pulls it to where surprise or shock
shatters the mirror I hide behind my back.

Perfect colophon: careful prescription
or serious warning, country cousin
to the main characters, embodied spirits
who steal center stage, demand my attention.

Read to the book's final page, feel its weight
in both hands. Breathe
the vegetable scent of inks
and know this: every letter counts.

FROM

About Little Charlie Lindbergh

(San Antonio: Wings Press, 2014)

Preface

Nineteen-thirty-six. I hurried as always
but was late. Eight centuries
or ten thousand years,
my small story fixed to my back.
Food came weighed and wrapped,
shelter engorged as surplus.

My own, my own, my own
was a mantra I could sing
in any season.
I could be who I was
and also anyone else.

I was late and also much too early,
came to justice
before its time.
Unprepared to receive me,
its rough grasp hurt my hand,
embedded its promises in my flesh.

Juggling gender
I was early and also late.
Juggling children, service,
my explosion of words
on stone, parchment,
or floating cyber cloud.

Only poetry and love met me
where we laughed.
After so many false starts
they came in whole and sure
before the finish line.

My hand fit the ancient print,
a radius of living settled
on my shoulders.
I am lunar standstill now,
calendar of hope.

It is 2018, and I discover
I am perfectly on time.
Soon I will disappear
together with all my kind,
and the earth
with its synchronized clock
will wake some blue-green morning
its rhythms safe for a while.

My Country

At this hour of winter north my country uncurls from sleep.
She moves in and out of a dream
where the Southern Cross plays close to the horizon.
That configuration of stars caresses her thighs
while keeping close their fading light.
My country is grumpy, reluctant to greet another day.

Storms assail one arthritic shoulder, monster storms
mythic before the moment of catastrophe.
Purposefully garbled language screeches in her ears.
She tries to repel the din, wipe rheumy sorrow
from the corners of her eyes, lure memory
and banish the ghosts that linger in her stiffened joints.

As sun warms, she covers her ears against a chorus
defying reflection, sworn enemies,
each out-shouting the other, each long ago
having forgotten that small kernel of meaning:
pure knowledge and intention of youth.
Exhaustion threatens. Only belligerence remains.

She tries to remember red stone buttes, Appalachian harmonies,
Harlem blues, the buffalo and a railroad to freedom.
She calls out to Crazy Horse and Harriet, Monk, Adrienne,
Popé and that secret place off-limits to all perpetrators.
Every woman and man
who ever stood against the tide.

My country shivers where she lingers bedside,
knob-kneed, soles seeking purchase
on the cold planks of this new day.

Alone and burning with fever, she discovers
they have stolen her dignity,
the thousand masks she wore with joyful pride.

My country falls back to bed aware the virus is fatal.
She tries to conserve the strength
she knows she may still need,
searches for a writing instrument
and something on which to scribble
a few sure words no one may ever read.

Joining of No Return

Where rock meets rock along the jagged cleft
above Pueblo Bonito's back wall,
where brick floats upon mythic emptiness
in Hagia Sophia's great dome,
where calligraphy becomes art
when image is forbidden above the entranceway
to an abandoned *caravansarai*
and the Silk Road sorts its memories,
there is a joining of no return.

Nothing messy about these seams,
nothing left over.
A waning sun turns the Nile's expanding ripples
to brief ridges of copper light
as sun turns wave fields on the Mekong,
Irrawaddy or Colorado the same haunting hue.
Yet all waves belong only to themselves
and along the lines where each river laps its shore
a line separates seeing from unknowing.

Such borders drip salt on slightly parted lips,
images embed themselves
in age-mottled flesh.
Great stones placed by the Inca
in perfect harmony
issue words I feared I might forget.
Each migration held by invisible mortar
imprints itself upon this landscape
unfolding on my tongue.

Where your skin and mine knit tight
between your right breast
and my left,
our bodies fit together perfectly,
and despite our sudden hot-flash blooms
touch speaks its language of years.
Here every cell brings memory home,
every nerve ending rests
at the boundary along which we grow.

Da Vinci's Proportions

Anti-Vitruvian, we revel
in the messy leftovers
after Leonardo's circle and square
conquer millennial thinking.

When life is no longer made
to fit well-oiled principles,
all maps can be redrawn,
all joys are possible.

About Little Charlie Lindbergh

The truth about little Charlie Lindbergh's
murder?
A hero's dark love of eugenics,
President Kennedy's lone killer,
or the Tonkin Gulf incident:
ghosts that still haunt us
pushing fantasy as fact
or fact as fantasy.

A year before I was born, Mother
gave birth to her first daughter,
named Margaret
and dead within hours.
I too am Margaret.
She always said she was pregnant
with me eighteen months.

Throughout her long life
she repeated
that other Margaret's name
and the story of her birth and death
until once, toward the end,
she turned to me in mock surprise
and asked
How could you think such a thing?
You have the wildest imagination!

A gesture here, comment there,
years of disparate clues
slipped between my anxious fingers
or lodged themselves in doubt.

The twin name unraveled.
The mysterious death remained.

Facts erased in a moment,
then reinforced:
Mother's fear of illness—
the common cold
but also quieter hidden ills,
unseen and menacing.

Pressing my brother
not to date
the college sweetheart
whose sister was rumored
to be mentally ill.
Fear of the raucous gene
compounding a shadowy blight.

I'd point out the mental illness
rife in our family as in many.
For Mother,
if no one saw
it wasn't there.

Grandfather just a dreamy old man.
Grandma's biting petulance,
her lies.
Uncle took a drink too many
but wasn't an alcoholic.
Never giving in to his gay identity:
all of it choice, not tragedy.

No wooden ladder remains standing
against the open second-story window

of a New Jersey mansion
in my family history.

No grassy knoll
obscures another script.
No fabricated strike
authorized a war
that would claim two million lives
and usher in the right to first attack.

My family secrets were humbler,
easier to hide.
They shaped individual
rather than collective lies.
They only made me crazy,
didn't seed posttraumatic stress
among nations.

His Name was Emmett Till,
His Name was Trayvon Martin

His name was Emmett Till, fourteen,
—friends called him Bobo
because of his stutter—
down from Chicago
to the town of Money, Mississippi,
running in the delta with his cousins.

Double-bubble, please ma'am,
at the neighborhood grocer.
They said he whistled
at the pretty white woman,
already fancied himself a man.

The crackers who kidnapped,
beat and murdered him,
hung fifty pounds of steel
around his neck
before throwing him in the Tallahatchie,
never believing they'd do time.

Laughing into their spittoons,
boasting of their exploit
in every backwoods backroom bar,
sold their story to Look Magazine
for $4,000. Serious sport.

Fifty-eight years later,
George Zimmerman
didn't need a white robe
to hunt down Trayvon Martin
in the soft rain of Sanford, Florida.

The neighborhood watchman
defied police orders
to stay in his car,
took refuge in Stand Your Ground,
harassed the young man
until he had to defend himself,
then shot him at close range.

Emmett and Trayvon, so close
in age, both executed
by white vigilantes
who lust to murder black children
—no other way to say this—
and 58 years
haven't changed the equation.

Emmett, Trayvon, and all black children
in between
whose faces didn't make
the 5 o'clock news
but dared to believe
they had a right to live.

It's the little things
lodge in my heart:
Emmett's bubble gum,
the *Skittles* Trayvon
bought to share
while watching the game
he never got to see.

And those mysteries
we will never know:
the precise moment
light goes out

in the eyes of a dying child,
the intimate sound
his secrets make
as they splinter against the wall.

This Poem's Got a Problem

This poem's got a problem,
an issue you might say
—mouthing linguistic dodge—
where vague carries the day
avoiding definition.

This poem wants to serve,
provoke chuckles
even outright laughter,
transmit the magic
of a charmed life.

But it slips from my grasp,
wanders under the railway bridge
where a family of seven
takes scant cover from the cold.
It notices hunger.

My poem takes an autumn walk
along the riverbank,
admires the gold-red turn
of Cottonwood leaves
until its morning calm

is split by the screams
of a woman forced
into the nearby woods:
some broken man
believes he has the right.

My poem tries to take refuge
in news or entertainment

(one and the same these days)
but today's school shooting
floods the screen.

On the other side of the world
27 members of a wedding party
are vaporized
because a novice recruit in Idaho
mistook them for enemy troops.

I am an optimist, light-hearted
and believe it or not
have a sense of humor,
but my poetry insists
on recording what it sees.

Margaret, 2006, at Frida Kahlo's house, Mexico City.
Photograph by Ximena Mondragón.

Margaret, 2008, with a copy of *Stones Witness*.
Photograph by Christina Frain.

Margaret, 2016, at Bihl Haus Arts, San Antonio, Texas.
Photograph by Mary G. Milligan

Margaret, 2017, San Francisco, California.
Photogrpah by Scott Brayley.

FROM

She Becomes Time

(San Antonio: Wings Press, 2016)

Time's Language

Light does not get old: a photon that emerged from
the Big Bang is the same age today as it was then.
There is no passage of time at light speed.
—Brian Greene

Time appears in its loose-fitting shift,
knocks on the child's windowpane,
hopscotches gleefully
then drags itself across the floor
for the unbearable wait.

Midlife it sizzles, careens against walls,
stumbles over roadblocks
trying out new dance steps
but catching its voluminous cloak
on all that excess furniture.

In age I hardly notice its devious passage,
steady breath lifting me through night.
Caressing my shoulders it launches
the occasional taunt
or hides in a double take of mirrors.

Sometimes it catches me off guard, sometimes
I want to tell it: *slow down, dammit!*
Sometimes I nestle in its arms
and understand its tempo
perfectly.

Look Up

Somersaulting across canyon slots
flying wall to wall
carrying sheets of desert varnish
to drape from narrow ledges
where ancestors stored corn
for winter's uncertainty.

Against those silent walls
you still see bodies
within bodies,
snake or lightning bolt,
mountain sheep in profile,
proud horns aligned for the fight.

Perhaps this is where you
are meant to look up,
turn left,
wedge your own body
from toe and finger hold
into a single perfect maneuver,

the one that will take you back 1300 years
to where they breathed,
worked, laughed
inside a circle of world
where the stitches sewing sky to earth
fail us now.

What misstep ripped time's seam,
tearing solution
from cause and effect,

placed multiple choices
in our hands
when two were more than enough?

When did time begin to move
faster than cosmic cycles,
a new story beginning
before its predecessor
had a chance to stop, rest,
remember its name?

When I Give Myself to Jungles

Do I hurt language, twist or offend it
in memory's house
when it shrieks
and I will not hold its hand?

Does verbing a noun or breathing
through imprisoned breast
risk my ribcage
in this time of war and gardens?

I sleep and glyphs etched in limestone
rise beside my bed
telling stories in words I can only hear
when I give myself to jungles.

Does Being Dead Make It Hard to Keep Up?

Between Roller Coaster and Cliff Hanger
Copernicus seemed distracted.
Hard to tell if he was put off
by my twenty-first century attire
or mind's poor reach.

Both our lives straddled centuries,
his fifteenth to sixteenth,
mine twentieth to twenty-first.
But he was man, I woman,
he a scientist and I a poet.

I complimented him on discovering
our planet is not unique
in the universe, then introduced him
to the provocative multiverse
just in case being dead

makes it hard to keep up
with the latest frontiers in his field.
I thought my contribution
might get him to open up and talk
or at least join me on this carnival ride.

I told him these days we know
it all comes down
to four concepts:
matter and energy interacting
in an arena of space and time.

Not just where we are in space,
but when we are in time.
I warned we are plagued
with fundamentalists as dangerous
as the Church that threatened him.

At last he turned to look at me,
benevolent understanding
in his deep brown eyes,
right index finger pressed to lips.
He smiled.

I know, he said, but you and I
inhabit different space
in different time.
You have enough answers now,
just not enough questions.

She Becomes Time

for Barbara

As she touches the boundary of time
she becomes time.
What is required of us at any moment,
unannounced, beyond pain or question.

As she settles against the mirror surface
she becomes a thousand versions
of herself,
every imprint she contains.

As she notices what grows between words
she moves from discomfort to terror
and back,
from breakdown to anticipation.

Her artist's hand pushes pathways
across the paper's surface,
creates spaces of silence
and spaces where secrets scream.

We grip hands so the knowing can flow
unobstructed through one to the other,
folding time and waiting
in braided fingers:

precisely here, precisely now.

Two-Step Sonnet

written for The People's State of the Union *Project*

I sit beneath the tree of promises, some
hanging dead on weighted boughs,
the mouths of others upturned
and open, hoping for rain.
Neighbors and strangers
crowd with me beneath the tree,
its shade broadens to embrace us all.

The tree of promises
promises nothing,
it is only a tree.
A girlchild with ancient eyes
leads us in song.
Everyone hears familiar language:
bones rattle down an unfamiliar scale.

Another *State of the Union* promises peace
as it secrets war, promises freedom
to those who brave desert death,
welcomes professional killers home
while deportations increase,
mourns another black youth dead,
shot by the cop who knows he has permission.

We the people have been through this
more than once. But the poem sounds,
its words create cacophonous harmony.
A century changes gender.
Tomorrow says no more war.

Another Night of Dreams

The elephant in the room seemed docile and clean
although immense.
I wondered what would happen
when he pooped.

I was making bread, kneading it comforted,
but became concerned
when instead of rising
the ball of dough shrank to walnut size.

My eyeglasses showed a jagged black crack
top to bottom.
I was relieved when you carefully peeled it off
with tweezers.

Another night of dreams
I want to slap upside the head.

I Am Waiting

for Lawrence Ferlinghetti, at 96,
and inspired by his poem of the same name.

I am waiting for my country
to catch up with its past,
that forgotten past
before it decided land-robs
and slave ships were good ideas.

I am waiting for my country
to stop lording it over
other countries because
they don't vote like we do
or we want their oil.

I am waiting for our keepers
of law and order to stop killing
kids because they're black,
because they wield toy guns
or fear.

I am waiting for waterboarding
to be judged as illegal as Twinkies,
a Sunday bath in Massachusetts
or gay sex in Oklahoma, Kansas,
Kentucky, Texas.

I used to wait for formidable breasts,
a graceful neck, and hair streaming
about my shoulders, not sprouting
from astonished body parts.
Too late for that.

Now I am waiting for my country
to honor poets and poetry,
send us our Christmas bonuses
because they love our poems,
Wall Street as example and mentor.

I am waiting right here right now
for a police van in rainbow hues
to roll up to the courtroom door
carrying Bush and Cheney
to the trial of their lives,

waiting for a child's face
in the crosshairs
to compel the man with the gun
to put it down
or refuse to pick it up,

where poverty, hunger, fear
of difference, and war
exist only in free museums
where teachers take children
to learn about back in the day.

I am waiting and waiting.
At 78, time is silver-blue
streaked with dark red.
I know the red will turn to blood
when 80 shrouds my shoulders.

I waited to be able to marry the woman
I love in an act more official
than the one we invented
28 years before. Impossible as
it seemed, today we have the pictures.

I waited and waited for my country
to speak to Cuba and, lo
and behold, today
they are whispering:
long-estranged lovers in a cold woods.

So I will keep waiting
as long as I'm here,
and keep on writing
these poems
with no bonus in the mail,

keep on breathing in and out,
licking the thin blanket
of melting frost
threatening to overtake
my moving lips.

When Justice Felt at Home

Something has changed.
Only old friends,
those who shared split peas
and white rice
on sweltering Havana nights
still call me *compañera*:
sweet designation
meaning comrade or friend
lover or familiar
in those luminous days
when justice felt at home
in our desire.

Now, more often than not,
it's *señora*:
regression to a prehistory
when married or single
young or old
mattered most.

Still, *compañera* and *compañero*
are indelibly embossed
on the swaying trunks of Royal Palms,
in Sierra Maestra granite
and along the dissembling coastline
of an Island that still shouts freedom
into gale-force winds.

FROM

The Morning After: Poetry and Prose in a Post-Truth World

(San Antonio: Wings Press, 2017)

Benoit Sees the Shapes

A quiet moment, yet we continue to marvel at its elegance.
Amused, Euclid laments no longer possessing
the breath to emit a joyous gasp.
He recognizes his smooth cones and spheres
have grown rough edges,
dance into ever smaller fingers reaching for the promised land.

Benoit Mandelbrot remembers the moment that changed his life
and ours. *I saw how the shapes came together,* he says,
(emphasis on *saw*), knows our language of words
cannot describe that other language he traces
until he shows us clouds and leaves,
shorelines and sand dunes chewed by wind and rain.

I love you, you tell me and no limits stalk our reckoning
as our fingers trace a line
between flesh and knowledge,
cellular memory and this field:
we are at once here and everywhere,
ancient patterns blooming on our skin.

To glimpse, see, then be able to teach draws wonder
from the heart while images of dying children
capture each nightly news cycle
and weapon-grade anything refuses to go down
in the history books as progress, only a sad detour
hastening our journey to that place of no return.

I want to trust Benoit's magical moment, Euclid's sanity,
Frida's double helix as I take your fingers into my heart
and hold them against our age.

I want to forget the contest itself leads to oblivion
and end this poem in hope
even as the evidence tries to stare me down.

Perhaps and Maybe

for Bob Holman

I woke this morning thinking about two words: PERHAPS and MAYBE. They bobbed behind my half-closed eyes, outlined in thick Rouault-like black lines. Twins, but not identical. The first is cool and collected. If it had a color, it would be blue, or a tasteful blue-green. Of course it does have a color. All words, letters, sounds and numbers have colors to me.

My off-the-top-of-my-head definition of PERHAPS is to introduce a sliver of uncertainty into a statement, as in "perhaps I will finish the job today," while at the same time leaving little doubt that the job will get done, giving me some wiggle room I guess. Intention dressed in elegance, calm around the edges.

MAYBE, on the other hand, is candy-cane red. Commonplace. Teasing, taunting. "Yes, no, maybe so." Like the ditty or song a child might sing while skipping rope or playing jacks or hopscotch. "Are you going to tell her today?" "Well, maybe." You know no more now than before you asked the question.

Adverbs aren't as powerful as nouns or verbs. Whole languages exist without them, and you could probably make yourself understood in a desperate attempt to speak another's language without ever using one. Adverbs signal degree rather than action or event. No one would call them necessary, or even exciting.

The online New Oxford American Dictionary defines PERHAPS as "used to express uncertainty or possibility: *perhaps I should have been frank with him*. Used when one does not wish to be too definite or assertive in the expression of an opinion." You hold the opinion, no question about that. But don't be too threatening in the way you put it out there. The first example given is: *perhaps not surprisingly, he was cautious about committing himself.* Perhaps not surprisingly: an ambiguous way of saying something if ever there was one. Used when making a polite request, offer, or suggestion: *would you perhaps consent to act as our guide?* In other words, more about form than content. Haltingly superfluous.

The same dictionary defines MAYBE more straightforwardly: "Perhaps; possibly: *maybe I won't go back \ maybe she'd been wrong to accept this job.*" Also lists it as a noun: *no ifs, buts, or maybes.*

Both words date to late Middle English, fifteenth century or so.

Faced with a job prospect, marriage proposal or offer of food when hungry, it's unlikely you'll hear a response involving either word. Yes would be expected. Or no in either of the first two cases if that's appropriate. In some cultures, hospitality questions—particularly those regarding the offering of food—must be responded to negatively at least twice before politely accepting. A custom designed to prevent the taker from appearing overly eager. Just as the guest is obligated to refuse, the host or hostess is obliged to insist, until the requisite back and forth has run its course.

In other cultures, questions are asked that may seem strange or insulting to outsiders. In Vietnam, for example, at first meeting women are interrogated as to age and how many children they have. Any response is acceptable, except that childlessness is considered sad.

Online information is meant to be condensed, reduced to minimal expression like the emoticons and 144-character tweets so rapidly taking over mainstream communication. So I decide to dig deeper. The Compact Oxford English Dictionary (COED, New Edition, 1991) is a compendium of words and definitions assembled in such minuscule type you can only read it with the aid of the powerful magnifying glass sold with it. Each book page is composed of nine smaller pages and each of these has three columns. Slightly more than halfway through the volume (book page 1310, small page 548), five paragraphs are devoted to PERHAPS.

After telling us it is an adverb, and explaining that in vulgar or careless speech the word has often been shortened to p'raps, it informs us that it appears only three times in the Bible of 1612, all in the New Testament and all in the Rhemish version. That's the thing about going to scholarly source texts: you are encouraged to do more research, in this case find out what makes the Bible of 1612 a reference, and what Rhemish is. Turns out, there was no Bible of 1612. Sixteen eleven is the year in which the King James version of the Bible was written, and it was published that year. Rhemish refers to the French city of Reims, a location that played an important role in Christian political history.

Perhaps without meaning to, this entry also reveals COED's bias: toward Western Christian civilization. The dictionary doesn't situate its word origins by referencing Muslim or Buddhist texts, or tell us the equivalents in cultures such as Aztec or Khmer. Think about it. And about how we are shaped by where we come from and where we go with our questions.

Only after getting these bits of information out of the way, does COED inform us that PERHAPS is "a word qualifying a statement so as to express possibility with uncertainty." Possibility with uncertainty. Now I know why I have been drawn to the word, with its perfect balance between what is possible and what may or may not happen. It is up to me, or you, to make it happen. Or keep it from happening. Either way, our will is involved.

Life's exquisite challenge.

Further down the column of infinitesimal print, definition B is worth quoting in full: "A statement qualified by 'perhaps,' an expression of possibility combined with uncertainty, suspicion, or doubt; an avowedly doubtful statement." Now suspicion has been added to uncertainty and our perfect balance has been pushed to cliff's edge. It has become a mystery, subject to the vagaries of chance or unknown forces. I am beginning to understand it is these hidden meanings folded into the word PERHAPS that give it its allure, much like the images half-obscured within the glyphs we see and that so firmly grab our imagination on Mayan stone. What is folded within something else. What speaks to us from beneath the surface. What will never let us believe we know it all.

On COED's page 1051 (small page 503), stuck between may-apple and may-bug, the word may-be or MAYBE is also listed as an adverb. Definition A refers us to "possibly, perhaps." Before assuming this is all I get, I read further and discover it is "sometimes used as a conjunction with a dependent *that*." And, more interestingly, that it is also common in the phrase "And I don't mean maybe." In other words: I am positive, sure. This arrogance may be MAYBE'S principle claim to fame.

In fact, after these dictionary definitions I am ready to explore what PERHAPS and MAYBE mean to me, why I opened my eyes this morning with both words clamoring for attention, begging to be taken seriously. It must be about choice, I think, the way I have always fought for options and emphasized, with other women in particular, how limiting it will be if we accept at face value only those which society offers us.

It will be of primary importance, I tell younger women especially, to understand there are other choices: more than you can imagine, unexpected, strange-looking, surprising. Choices that may not fit neatly with the expectations you have been taught to believe are inevitable. The best evidence against ideas involving fate or destiny.

Play with dolls or construction sets. Go with protocol or with your feelings. Let that boy kiss you or resign yourself to being an outcast.

Or, let that girl kiss you. Or kiss her. Find a man or remain what the patriarchy disdainfully calls a spinster. You're your body inside or outside the marriage contract. Identify as male or female or anyone else along our human arc. Be a mother and an artist. Sell out or not sell at all. Go to war or let them destroy us. Make a profit or save the planet. Forget or remember. Grow old and stay young, accepting both conditions joyously.

Any child, given the freedom to explore her instincts will come up with dozens of alternative equations, rejecting the confines of our binary world. Perhaps this is the real difference between cyber-speak and human-speak: we are made of more than zeroes and ones.

The Translation Project

Written after selecting the poets and
their poems, writing the introduction
and translating the texts for
Only the Road / Solo el camino:
Eight Decades of Cuban Poetry.

First I chose the poets, then their poems.
The map where I walked grew
transparent then dense as Precambrian rock.
It was winter but the words themselves
stumbled across thresholds
carrying the weightlessness
of spring.

The silvery-blue number fourteen loomed
until its one and its four
switched places,
danced close to slow music
then abandoned themselves
to the rhythms of *cumbia*
and *guaguancó*.

A door opened revealing another door
and another, mixed metaphors
dissolving in smoky mirrors
where images collapse
beneath the weight
of so many questions.
I follow every one.

Where I huddled with him and all his tribe
only her truth was audible
Words flew in from another century
and I deciphered their porcelain music
ignoring dirty blankets
seeded with an invisible danger
I knew could do me in.

Her voice discharged its hormones
in three-quarter time
and I found them piled behind a door
unopened for fifty years.
You, standing beside
this pillar of salt,
threatened to take my last breath.

You over there fought me until, exhausted,
I gave up and let you have your way.
Half the foreseeable future was Royal palms
and a coastline pretending to be
wall or direction
battered by strange creatures
bearing guns and shields.

I dissembled her wit and his suicide gasp,
then rebuilt each in its register,
refusing to let them sleep.
Her quiet irony, his broken rage,
your last line and the silence
between your syllables
echo only themselves.

Their ears hold another language now,
identical yet entirely different,
recognize legacy
as their mouths emit strange sounds
where readers from a country
none of them know
pay homage to perfect pitch.

The Morning After

To the children

It's the morning after and the polar bear
licks blood
from his foot's white fur.
Ice is jagged and cuts, its islands recede
to the beat of human denial.
Far to the south: a dying parrot's heart cries.

It's the morning after and beneath the wall
long scarring our southern border
tunnels carry *coyotes* and their human cargo
while real coyotes and smaller animals
burrow for daily bread, unaware
of a madman's ravings, pompous threat.

It's the morning after. I wish there was a pill.
So many hard-won battles tremble
on this map redrawn by hatred's hand.
The Bully in Chief stands before us:
triumphant, tricked by the deceptive weave
of his Emperor's New Clothes.

It's the morning after and emergency rooms
fill with attempted suicides:
queer teenager, black youth, young girl
who hoped her ceiling would begin to crack,
boy whose brother was murdered by the cop
still riding his neighborhood patrol.

Six-year-old Maia tells her mother *Wake me*
when Hillary wins. The next morning
she is afraid to go to school:
If we speak Spanish in the street,
she wants to know,
will they send us away?

It's the morning after. Shock subsides
to fear and rage
throughout the world.
But beware of an elite
still measuring loss by lies and votes,
unable to hear the real stories:

It's the morning after, one of many. Listen
to the heartland's threatened factory,
another child who wakes up hungry,
love too afraid to speak its name
or the single mother of three
without a home.

Trust me rings hollow on the liar's lips.
I will fix it isn't the answer.
Only together can we resist:
by loving, creating,
and embracing the vulnerable among us
four more years.

Beneath a Trespass of Sorrow
(San Antonio: Wings Press, 2014)
Miniature chapbook

Bodies / Shields
(San Antonio: Wings Press, 2015)
Miniature chapbook

Uncollected Poems

A Season with No Visible Exit

*You must have talked a lot
with your death...*
–Juan Gelman, "Paco"

This balmy day, air claims the word *caress*
inhabiting both warp and weft
while sharp needles of ice
dagger my memory,
more premonition than warning.

In the bone chill cold of a season
with no visible exit,
I read *Paco* in the title of your poem
and wonder if knowing which Paco
makes a difference.

Urondo familiar in memory,
immense in tribute, historic
in a history that ended badly
but no less heroic, historic
in a time pressed close to breast.

Breath Carries Unwavering Meaning

I know I am asking a lot of the poem
sent out on currents of fouled air
in this time of devious deregulation.

I am aware my words may feel lonely
among so many alternate facts,
presidential tweets crowding cyberspace.

What can a word do, or a series of words
strung together in urgent hope?
So much command and cliché to overcome.

But possibility explodes, pyrotechnic flowers
lighting up this deadened sky
of all-consuming rhetoric.

Mouth opens, throat clears, breath carries
unwavering meaning
through an almost silent spring.

Exile (Details)

Dreaming, she walks from the corner of the park
to just before the old bookstore,
even when she tries to reenter sleep
wakes before she gets there,
cannot arrive.

She is born again and again,
small births and great
move each new chapter:
a Rubix Cube
in slow motion.

Chunks of sidewalk and knowing faces
lift moments from her waking life,
wrench them from hand and mouth.
In this other place
where words cut her tongue,

taste flees it: pieces of a puzzle
she cannot complete.
Ketchup forever an imposter
when remembering Chimichurri,
meats sliced against the grain.

She is reborn until she loses count
of before and after,
right hand from left,
an anthem no longer remembered
word for word.

Twenty years later this nation will
still be other, and she will tire
of telling those born here
stories of the nation she once inhabited,
also other then.

Great Grandson

He is curious, at a year and a half
pulls every book from the shelf,
turns pages, makes sounds
that are surely words,
watches and grins.

We struggle to give him a world
he can demolish, reorder
and make anew, knowing
our legacy doesn't work
for everyone.

Our only option now: to bequeath
imperfection, turmoil where dis-
ease makes its faltering stand
and he forgives
the error of our ways.

Or perhaps, and I will be long gone
by then, he will write a poem
like this to his great grandchild
he hopes may still be able
to take its desperate turn.

Time's Perfect Duet

On Tuesday 14 minutes melted
along with spring snow
unexpected but not impossible
at the end of April.

I am missing almost two hours
that disappeared as I flew
from Albuquerque to New York.
True, the flight began at midnight
and landed at LaGuardia the following dawn.

Should I be looking at confused time zones
or hungry memory, voracious
as it ticks off each box
accounting for this blurred loss.

What of the seconds disappearing
through pleats of mind
or falling between fingertips
that only hope to dress and undress
when no one's looking.

Time like discreet views through
the moving window
of a 1941 Ford.
The child believes the scenery
moves before her watchful eyes
while the landscape knows

it is the girl who will become a woman
then an old woman

and, finally, a very old woman
bringing into perfect balance

the car's speed, window's laughter,
landscape unfolding
and time's perfect duet
keeping each where it
works its magic.

Untended Evidence

A trickle of sleep from just beside the tear duct
stops halfway down my cheek.
Ribbons in clashing colors, but really:
what colors clash?
Mexican blues and greens, oranges
and reds, have always been friends.
A thought that lifts or batters
depends upon the season.
Winter's letters cut like freshly sharpened knives.
He says he is going home
but makes a long detour: nothing is sacred, after all.
She confesses to nothing.
After all, with what she's seen
she knows *everything she writes will be used against her*
or against those she loves.
None of this evidence requires tending.
It grows wild
wherever you go.

Rendering It a Hat

How to make everyone forget who you are
by talking about it all the time.
How to make everyone remember
exactly who you are
by never mentioning it.
The it,
elephant in the room
or hidden within the Little Prince's drawing,
rendering it a hat to unimaginative eyes.
Proud, it shines on your skin.
No one can wash it away.
Every language does it honor.
Starring, finally,
as itself in the play.

Shapeshifter's Work

If Mother hadn't implored Father
I would have been
Margaret Reinthal,
Bat Mitzvah perhaps at 12 or 13,
accepting the liturgy
or writing a feminist Haggadah.

More likely I would have turned my back
on Jewish ritual
as I did on the Protestant clone
Mother was so sure
would erase all taint,
deliver America's salvation.

But fascism carved early resistance
into morality's flesh and bones.
Denial wears a different skin,
sings off-key
when six million crimes
shadow memory.

The shapeshifter's work cut out for me,
I became the woman
who knew where she must stand
but not how to get there.
Even today, convinced non-believer,
I trip over my own uncertain feet.

Hadron Collider of Imagination

That towering anvil, weather with the power
to push a flash flood
between narrow canyon walls
dragging branches and bodies in its path.

Spreading up and out on this horizon
of peaceful sand and sage
against calm blue sky the giant thunderhead
expands.

Within its fierce mystery shards of ancient pottery
modern wrist watches
and the prayers of generations
race in a Hadron Collider of imagination.

Letters of a lost alphabet in random disarray
a manatee's desire
a million sunsets in full bloom
and fruits so rare they have yet to be tasted.

Never doubt its swirling mass hides baby birds,
a coyote's plaintive song
or the somersaulting questions
of someone in the wrong place at the wrong time.

Triage

Meet this place where fast creeps up on you,
takes you by surprise
and you must go this way or that
without resorting to reason.

Triage sends poison darts beneath the nails
of outstretched fingers:
who to save and who leave
to climb her final mountain alone.

Triage occupies transparency where you
come face to face with yourself
or the person you love
more than you love yourself.

It requires a new stripe on the rainbow,
a teal never seen before:
blue greener than kindness, green
that will not seek refuge in forests.

It slips and slides in its own blood,
runs circles about you,
then tightens like a pillory for the kill,
defeating the breath in your lungs.

Choice rubs shoulders with clear evidence,
time's energy spent,
erosion's cycle clawing
at this threshold of depleted will.

Disgraced politicians or heaving gasps
of a planet battered to breaking,
morality remaining only in human hands
extended to take other hands.

Implore or let go, triage combs through hair
tangled with the sweat of centuries.
I hear you. I hold you.
I follow you to the horizon.

Made Rich by Art and Revolution

When I am gone and August comes
to my desert,
rain will soak sand,
its rich scent rising
to enter the lungs of another mother or walker,
someone whose intention and desire
I cannot know.

When I am gone this painting of little islands
miniature trees and birds
floating in a magical sea of blue
will hang in someone else's house.
Will that person tell the story
of poor Nicaraguan peasants
made rich by art and revolution?

A granddaughter may inherit
my turquoise earrings.
The clay pans I've used for years,
their pungency filling the house,
will offer up a new generation
of bread.
Someone not yet born may read this poem.

But who will ask the questions
born of the answers
I juggle today.
Who will know the heat
of this great love,
or catch fragments of my memory
reassembling just before dawn.

About the Author

Margaret Randall is a feminist poet, writer, photographer and social activist. She is the author of over 100 books. Born in New York City in 1936, she has lived for extended periods in Albuquerque, New York, Seville, Mexico City, Havana, and Managua. Shorter stays in Peru and North Vietnam were also formative. In the 1960s, with Sergio Mondragón she founded and co-edited *El Corno Emplumado / The Plumed Horn,* a bilingual literary journal which for eight years published some of the most dynamic and meaningful writing of an era. Robert Cohen took over when Mondragón left the publication in 1968. From 1984 through 1994 she taught at a number of U.S. universities.

Randall was privileged to live among New York's abstract expressionists in the 1950s and early '60s, participate in the Mexican student movement of 1968, share important years of the Cuban revolution (1969-1980), the first three years of Nicaragua's Sandinista project (1980-1984), and visit North Vietnam during the heroic last months of the U.S. American war in that country (1974). Her four children— Gregory, Sarah, Ximena and Ana—have given her ten grandchildren and two great-grandchildren. She has lived with her life companion, the painter and teacher Barbara Byers, for the past 31 years.

Upon her return to the United States from Nicaragua in 1984, Randall was ordered to be deported when the government invoked the 1952 McCarran-Walter Immigration and Nationality Act, judging opinions expressed in some of her books to be "against the good order and happiness of the United States." The Center for Constitutional Rights defended Randall, and many writers and others joined in an almost five-year battle for reinstatement of citizenship. She won her case in 1989.

In 1990 Randall was awarded the Lillian Hellman and Dashiell Hammett grant for writers victimized by political repression. In 2004 she was the first recipient of PEN New Mexico's Dorothy

Doyle Lifetime Achievement Award for Writing and Human Rights Activism.

Recent non-fiction books by Randall include *To Change the World: My Life in Cuba* (Rutgers University Press), *More Than Things* (University of Nebraska Press), *Che On My Mind,* and *Haydée Santamaría, Cuban Revolutionary: She Led by Transgression* (both from Duke University Press). Her most recent nonfiction works are *Only the Road / Solo el Camino: Eight Decades of Cuban Poetry* (Duke, 2016) and *Exporting Revolution: Cuba's Global Solidarity* (Duke, 2017).

"The Unapologetic Life of Margaret Randall" is an hour-long documentary by Minneapolis filmmakers Lu Lippold and Pam Colby. It is distributed by Cinema Guild in New York City.

Randall's most recent collections of poetry and photographs are *Their Backs to the Sea* (2009), *My Town: A Memoir of Albuquerque, New Mexico* (2010), *As If the Empty Chair: Poems for the Disappeared / Como si la silla vacía: poemas para los desaparecidos* (2011), *Where Do We Go from Here?* (2012), *Daughter of Lady Jaguar Shark* (2013), *The Rhizome as a Field of Broken Bones* (2013), *About Little Charlie Lindbergh and other Poems* (2014), *Beneath a Trespass of Sorrow* (2014), *Bodies / Shields* (2015), *She Becomes Time* (2016), and *The Morning After: Poetry and Prose in a Post-Truth World* (2017), all published by Wings Press. In October of 2017, she was awarded the prestigious Medal of Literary Merit by Literatura en el Bravo, Chihuahua, Mexico.

For more information about the author, visit her website at www.margaretrandall.org.

About the Editors

Katherine M. Hedeen's latest book-length translations include *night badly written* (Action Books) and *tasks* (coimpress, long-listed for the Best Translated Book Award, shortlisted for the National Translation Award, 2017) by Víctor Rodríguez Núñez, and *Nothing Out of This World* (Smokestack), an anthology of contemporary Cuban poetry which won the English PEN Award. She is the Poetry Translation Editor for the *Kenyon Review* and the recipient of two NEA Translation Project Grants. She is a Professor of Spanish at Kenyon College.

Víctor Rodríguez Núñez (Havana, 1955) is a poet, journalist, literary critic, translator, and scholar. He has published fifty books of poetry throughout the Americas, Europe, and Asia, and his work has received many major awards in the Spanish-speaking world, most recently, Spain's coveted Loewe Poetry Prize. He has compiled three anthologies that define his poetic generation, as well as another of 20th century Cuban poetry, *La poesía del siglo XX en Cuba* (2011). He has brought out various critical editions, introductions, and essays on Spanish American poets. One of Cuba's most outstanding contemporary writers, he divides his time between Gambier, Ohio, where he is Professor of Spanish at Kenyon College, and Havana.

About the Cover Artist

L iliana Wilson was born in Valparaíso, Chile. Her early paintings sought to process the trauma she had witnessed in Chile that coincided with dramatic political changes following the election of Salvador Allende and the subsequent 1973 military coup that initiated a wave of human rights violations. She immigrated to the United States in 1977 and pursued studies in art at Texas State University. A book on her work called *Ofrenda* was published by Texas A&M Press in 2015, edited by Dr Norma E. Cantú. *Ofrenda* is a collection of writings on Liliana's work by Gloria Anzaldúa and others. She has exhibited throughout the United States, Mexico, Argentina and Italy. Her latest work represent immigrants and refugees transitioning into unknown worlds. Occupying liminal spaces, they are portrayed en un viaje, a journey of integration toward wholeness—and arriving in new contextual spaces they can finally call home.

Wings Press was founded in 1975 by Joanie Whitebird and Joseph F. Lomax, both deceased, as "an informal association of artists and cultural mythologists dedicated to the preservation of the literature of the nation of Texas." Publisher, editor and designer since 1995, Bryce Milligan is honored to carry on and expand that mission to include the finest in American writing—meaning all of the Americas, without commercial considerations clouding the decision to publish or not to publish.

Wings Press intends to produce multi-cultural books, chapbooks, ebooks, recordings and broadsides that enlighten the human spirit and enliven the mind. Everyone ever associated with Wings has been or is a writer, and we know well that writing is a transformational art form capable of changing the world, primarily by allowing us to glimpse something of each other's souls. We believe that good writing is innovative, insightful, and interesting. But most of all it is honest. As Bob Dylan put it, "To live outside the law, you must be honest."

Likewise, Wings Press is committed to treating the planet itself as a partner. Thus the press uses as much recycled material as possible, from the paper on which the books are printed to the boxes in which they are shipped.

As Robert Dana wrote in *Against the Grain*, "Small press publishing is personal publishing. In essence, it's a matter of personal vision, personal taste and courage, and personal friendships." Welcome to our world.

Colophon

This first edition of *Time's Language: Selected Poems (1959-2018)* by Margaret Randall, edited by Katherine M. Hedeen and Víctor Rodríguez Núñez, has been printed on 55 pound Edwards Brothers "natural" paper containing a percentage of recycled fiber. Titles have been set in Bernhard Modern type, the text in Adobe Caslon type. This book was designed by Bryce Milligan.

On-line catalogue and ordering:
www.wingspress.com
Wings Press titles are distributed to the trade by the
Independent Publishers Group
www.ipgbook.com
and in Europe by Gazelle
www.gazellebookservices.co.uk

Also available as an ebook.